STANFORD UNIVERSITY PUBLICATIONS
UNIVERSITY SERIES

HISTORY, ECONOMICS, AND POLITICAL SCIENCE
VOLUME III   NUMBER 3

Oriental Crime in California

A Study of Offenses Committed by Orientals in That State 1900-1927

By

WALTER G. BEACH
Professor of Social Science

AMS PRESS
NEW YORK

TABLE OF CONTENTS

ACKNOWLEDGMENTS

The research the results of which are presented in these pages is the work of many hands. While the planning, the supervision, much of the writing, and certainly the responsibility for errors and defects are the principal author's, several others have shared in the study as a whole. In particular, credit is due Miss Margaret S. Gould, who organized and carried out the laborious field work, involving the gathering of facts and figures from the various prisons of the state. She also arranged the tables and wrote a first draft setting forth the more immediately evident aspects which they revealed. It was necessary then to examine this material more thoroughly, both in regard to its accuracy and in regard to its interpretations and their expression. Credit is due to Dr. W. H. Metzler and Mrs. Charles Norman for working through and correcting much of the statistical matter and for restating and clarifying many sentences and paragraphs, and to Mr. H. R. Skelton for a final laborious, painstaking, and thorough revision of all the statistics involved. Drs. C. N. Reynolds and R. T. LaPiere also read the manuscript and furnished many suggestions in regard to interpretation and statement.

W. G. B.

STANFORD UNIVERSITY, CALIFORNIA
March 10, 1932

Oriental Crime in California

I. INTRODUCTION

Scope of study.—It is desired in this study to ascertain the place which the Chinese and Japanese residents in California occupy in the records of crime committed in the state; and to note specifically the laws which they are prone to break and thus their typical or characteristic offenses against the law.

It is felt that this knowledge may indicate whether or not these races now domiciled here show any particular criminal tendencies, and that it may disclose the part which they contribute in the forming of the criminal element in the community. And since the Chinese and Japanese of the first generation are prohibited from participation in the political life of this country, we may perhaps ascertain whether or not any basis for this exclusion can be found in their conduct—whether or not they possess any peculiar anti-social characteristics which make them a danger to their fellowmen.

Method of investigation.—Official police records furnish the most trustworthy basis for a study of this nature. This avoids the dangers of inaccuracy inevitably involved in the assembling of reports or opinions from the press or from observing individuals; and the coloring of facts through prejudices is somewhat obviated, though it is impossible to measure the extent to which the activities of police authorities may be affected by prejudice. However, in so far as police prejudice exists it seems to be hostile rather than favorable to the Oriental, and therefore tends to increase the number of arrests.

The material for this study was assembled from the police blotters of the county and city police departments and from the record books of the penal institutions in the state.[1] Necessarily, in reference to arrests, only those centers were included from which relatively full records were obtainable. Two difficulties were encountered in this regard: some police departments had no records of arrests made in the early part of the century; others which had such records had no specifications regarding the nativity of the prisoner, and it was found that names could not be a guide in this case. It proved possible, however, to obtain a sufficiently uniform

---

[1] It is a pleasure to record that in the gathering of the data police officers were uniformly helpful in giving the investigators every facility at their command.

set of data pertinent to the plan we desired to follow, but it was not possible to secure equal uniformity in the time periods. The differences in the latter respect were not sufficient, however, to destroy the value of the study.

Reliance upon records of arrests calls for a word of explanation. Arrests are not equivalent to convictions. They do not necessarily involve an equal amount of weighing of evidence and so may be more subject to prejudice and error. It is quite probable that because of race discrimination arrests may be expected to be larger in number than in the case of the native white population. In so far as this is true it would lead to an exaggeration of the so-called crime record of the Orientals. Moreover, in making comparisons of crime records such as is done in this study, it should also be noted that city and county jails are places of punishment for minor offenses and that police blotters ordinarily state the disposal of the case. Perhaps the outstanding fact which this study brings to light is the very high percentage of arrests of Orientals for what are classed as minor offenses. These constitute the type of offenses the punishment for which is usually fine or brief inprisonment in jail. Hence, except for serious offenses, the disposal of which is revealed in the records of the state penitentiaries, the city and county police records of "arrests" are as near a comparative summary of offenses as can be obtained. It is fair to add that now and then there is a record of the arrest of a considerable number of Orientals—usually Chinese—on a single occasion without the disposition of the cases being stated. In such cases, it seems probable that a wholesale arrest of this sort was made, perhaps to satisfy public clamor or to make a showing of police activity, and that after a brief time those arrested were set free. All such multiple arrests are, of course, included in our data covering the jurisdictions and the periods designated.

The plan adopted was to secure data under the following heads:

1. The total number of Chinese and Japanese arrested in cities and counties, from 1900 to 1927
2. The nature of the offenses for which they were arrested
3. The occupation of each offender at the time of his or her arrest
4. The age of each offender at the time of his or her arrest
5. The ratio of Chinese and Japanese arrests to total number of arrests in each locality and period

In this way it was thought possible to learn (1) how many Chinese and Japanese were arrested annually, and to trace: (a) to what extent their law-breaking increased or decreased each year; (b) to what extent they figured in the total arrests. One could further deduce (2) what laws the Chinese and Japanese were prone to break, also wherein the one race differed from the other in this respect, and the light this might throw upon the relationship of each to general social life. By knowing the occupation of the offender, judgment may be possible as to (3) their industriousness or shiftlessness and, in conjunction with a knowledge of the character of their law-breaking, whether they tend to form a peculiarly dangerous or harmless element.

Knowledge of the ages of the offenders may throw light upon (4) the disposition toward crime of the young and the old and the relationship of this factor to the process of assimilation. Finally, a knowledge of the number and character of Oriental offenses, together with a knowledge of the total amount of crime in the state, should give an idea of (5) the criminality of the Chinese and Japanese, and by measuring this with their place in the volume of population, it may be possible to visualize to what extent they form a criminal element.

This last-named point can be more clearly adjudged when racial history and cultural characteristics also are considered. Such a consideration would relate the problem of criminality to cultural life and also to the culture-adjustment process which migration involves. To make adequate use of this point of view calls for a series of related studies upon other phases of Oriental-Occidental culture contact founded upon a broad knowledge of Chinese and Japanese cultural life. It has been possible in this research to consider only the more evident of these cultural aspects and to suggest their place in the fuller interpretation of special situations revealed in this study.

Status of Orientals in the United States.—Chinese and Japanese residents occupy a peculiar status in the United States. By law they are prevented from entering our country except under certain limited classifications such as travelers and students; and they may not become citizens by legal process. Yet, because of the relatively long history of Oriental immigration to the United States, during part of which freer entrance and permanent residence was possible, there is now a considerable Oriental population, the younger generation of which is native-born and so possesses the political and legal rights of other native-born citizens. Notwithstanding this fact, however, the entire group—first, second, and third generations alike—tends to be looked upon by white citizens as alien. For Oriental physical characteristics remain fixed and serve as marks which outweigh in the popular mind the inner or mental alterations brought about by the process of assimilation.[1]

This inability to change physical marks of race (except by amalgamation, which is legally forbidden in the states mainly concerned) has led to a degree of racial segregation of both Oriental peoples which gives them a

---

[1] This aspect of assimilation has been carefully discussed by Robert G. Park in Park and Burgess, *Introduction to the Study of Sociology,* and elsewhere.

peculiar position and undoubtedly is a factor in regard to any abnormal or criminal behavior observed. Segregation always seems to affect the cultural characteristics of a people, creating a mental bias and a social attitude which leads to greater or less abnormal behavior. The American Chinese and Japanese are neither American nor Oriental, and the consciousness of this situation, with its evident limitations upon vocation, residence, and social status, reacts upon their minds unfavorably, especially among the younger members.

Segregation, however, is more pronounced among the Chinese than among the Japanese and therefore has a different character and assumes a different importance in respect to social consequences. While it is not possible to determine how much weight should be given to it in regard to the behavior question, it seems probable that it is of large importance in explaining peculiarities of Chinese life in California. This topic is more fully explored in the concluding chapter of this study.

II. THE CHINESE AND JAPANESE IN CALIFORNIA

Before beginning an analysis of Chinese and Japanese arrests in California, it is important to see the fraction they constitute of the entire population of the state.

To California came first the Chinese and then the Japanese in large numbers. Owing to immigration conditions and legislation, the volume of their populations during the last forty years has changed in an irregular manner. After the Exclusion Act of 1882 the Chinese population began to dwindle, and owing to more agreeable arrangements for them the Japanese population began to increase.[1]

The comparison of the 1900 and 1920 census records of population shows these changes markedly: in 1900 there were 45,753 Chinese in the state; in 1910 the number had dropped to 36,248; and in 1920 it was only 28,812. The Japanese in 1900 were 10,151; in 1910 they had increased to 41,356; and in 1920 they numbered 71,952. From 1900 to 1920 the Chinese declined about 37 per cent, and the Japanese increased about 608 per cent.

During the same period, however, the general population of the state increased about 131 per cent: in 1900 the total population was 1,485,053; in 1910 the number was 2,377,549; and in 1920 it was 3,426,861.

With the steady gain in the numbers of the general population, the decline in the number of the Chinese down to 1920 made their place in the population rather insignificant. And even the seemingly large increase in the numbers of Japanese gave them only a modest position. In 1900 the Chinese formed 3.2 per cent of the total population in the state, in 1910 their proportion dropped to 1.5 per cent, and in 1920 they comprised but 0.8 per cent of the total population. The Japanese in 1900 were 0.7 per cent of the total population; in 1910 they had risen to be 1.7 per cent; and in 1920, though their numbers had increased from 41,356 to 71,952, their ratio to the total population in the state was but 2.1 per cent. So that on the basis of the figures for 1920 the Chinese constituted less than 1 per cent and the Japanese a fraction over 2 per cent of the entire population in the state.[2]

Table 1, which appears on the following page, exhibits these changes at a glance.

---

[1] Statements in this and the succeeding paragraphs are drawn from the *United States Census Report, 1920,* Vol. III, or *1910,* Vol. II.

[2] *United States Census Report, 1920,* Vol. III, p. 106.

TABLE 1

CHANGES IN GENERAL AND ORIENTAL POPULATION IN CALIFORNIA, 1900–1920

Population	In 1900		In 1910		In 1920	
	Number	Percentage	Number	Percentage	Number	Percentage
Total	1,485,053	100.0	2,377,549	100.0	3,426,861	100.0
Chinese	45,753	3.1	36,248	1.5	28,812	0.8
Japanese	10,151	0.7	41,356	1.7	71,952	2.1

Increase in Oriental female population.—The Oriental population in the country is composed somewhat largely of males. There is, however, a marked tendency toward increase in the proportion of females in California, especially among the Japanese. Better marital conditions and the larger number of children and young people point to the existence of an organized family life, with all the possibilities for more healthful development that this condition can afford. From this it may be presumed that more stability is now the rule among the Oriental settlers than formerly; the restless immigrant has now settled into normal life.

Considering separately the male and the female population in the state, the Chinese males at the present time constitute 1.3 per cent of the entire male population, and the Japanese, 2.5 per cent.[1] The decline in the Chinese population and the increase in the Japanese can be traced here: in 1900 the Chinese male population formed 5.2 per cent of the total male population in the state, in 1910 it was 2.5 per cent, and in 1920 it was 1.3 per cent. Among the Japanese in 1900 the males constituted 1.2 per cent of the total male population, 2.7 per cent in 1910, and 2.5 per cent in 1920.

The proportion of Oriental males in the state is seen more clearly by comparing the male Oriental figures with the male total in the general population. At the present time males constitute 84.1 per cent of the total Chinese population in the state, and 63.1 per cent of the total Japanese population in the state. The general male population constitutes 52.9 per cent of the total population in the state.

The proportion of the general male population has not greatly varied in the three decades; the percentage of the Chinese males has decreased with the decrease in Chinese total population and with the increase of Chinese females, maintaining, however, the highest ratio of male to female population in the state. The Japanese show a marked decrease in their pro-

---

[1] The figures quoted here and on the following pages are drawn from the *United States Census Report, 1920*, Vol. III, or *1910*, Vol. II. It has not seemed wise to use the *Census Report* for 1930, since the data gathered for this study do not reach that date.

TABLE 2

ORIENTAL MALE POPULATION IN CALIFORNIA, 1900–1920

Male Population	In 1900		In 1910		In 1920	
	Number	Percent-age	Number	Percent-age	Number	Percent-age
Total	820,531	55.2	1,322,978	55.7	1,813,591	52.9
Chinese	42,297	92.4	33,003	91.0	24,230	84.1
Japanese	9,598	94.6	35,116	84.9	45,414	63.1

portion of males to their total population, decreasing from 94.6 per cent in 1900 to 63.1 per cent in 1920, and thus approaching the general proportion of males in the state.

While the Chinese male population decreased from 1900 to 1920 by 18,743, or 56.4 per cent, the Chinese female population increased from 3,456 in 1900 to 4,582 in 1920, or 32.6 per cent. Among the Japanese the increase of females is more marked; in 1900 there were 553 females; this jumped to 6,240 in 1910, and to 26,538 in 1920, an increase of 4,700 per cent. The proportion that the Oriental females form of their total population is seen in the table below.

TABLE 3

ORIENTAL FEMALE POPULATION IN CALIFORNIA, 1900–1920

Female Population	In 1900		In 1910		In 1920	
	Number	Percent-age	Number	Percent-age	Number	Percent-age
Total*	664,522	44.7	1,054,571	44.4	1,613,270	47.1
Chinese	3,456	7.6	3,245	9.0	4,582	15.9
Japanese	553	5.4	6,240	15.1	26,538	36.9

* Figures given for total female population represent the number of white females, but not the total number of females in the state.

The Chinese female population increased from 7.6 per cent to 15.9 per cent of the total Chinese population in the state, and the Japanese female population increased from 5.4 per cent to 36.9 per cent of their total. This has brought about a change in the ratio of males to 100 females; among the Chinese the ratio has dropped from 1,223.9, in 1900, to 528.8 in 1920; and among the Japanese the ratio declined from 1,735.6 in 1900 to 171.1 in 1920, bringing the Japanese ratio of males to 100 females much nearer the level of the general ratio for the state, which is 112.4 in 1920, thus bespeaking for the Japanese a more nearly equal possibility for normal conditions of life.

TABLE 4

NUMBER OF MALES TO 100 FEMALES, IN
CALIFORNIA, 1900–1920

Population	In 1900	In 1910	In 1920
Total in state............	123.5	125.5	112.4
Chinese	1,223.9	1,017.0	528.8
Japanese	1,753.6	562.8	171.1

Marital conditions.—The Chinese population over 15 years of age in the state in 1910 was about evenly divided between married and single: 53.8 per cent were single, and 41.3 per cent were married.[1] Among the Japanese, 57.5 per cent were single and 39.7 per cent were married. This difference in marital condition between the two races may be explained by the fact that a considerable portion of the Japanese population, as can be seen below, are juveniles; this fact explains in part also their larger increase in female population, as due to the birth of female children in this country.

Table 5 illustrates the proportion of the married and single Orientals, by age groups.

TABLE 5

PERCENTAGE OF MARRIED AND SINGLE CHINESE AND
JAPANESE IN CALIFORNIA, 1910*

Age Group	Chinese		Japanese	
	Married	Single	Married	Single
15–24 years	9.8	89.5	3.5	95.8
25–44 years	54.4	41.4	33.2	65.1
45 and over	51.6	42.4	59.5	34.7
All ages 15 years and over	41.3	53.8	39.7	57.5

* Oriental marital condition by age groups is given in *Census Report, 1910*, but not in 1920.

Very few divorces are reported: in 1910 among the Chinese, 8, and among the Japanese, 45. The reason for this lies in the nature of their marriage tie, the status of their women, their religious precepts, and other elements of their culture.

---

[1] This is as reported to the census-taker; but how many of those reporting the married condition are living here in the single condition cannot be ascertained.

There are relatively more Chinese married in the younger age groups than Japanese. In the age group 15–24, the married Chinese are 9.8 per cent and the married Japanese only 3.5 per cent; in the group 25–44, the married Chinese are 54.4 per cent and the Japanese 33.2 per cent. But in the oldest age group, 45 and over, the Japanese percentage of the married population is higher, 59.5 per cent, as compared to the Chinese with 51.6 per cent; and in this group the proportion of single Chinese is higher than in the other groups: 42.4 per cent, to the Japanese 34.7 per cent. This may be explained by the constitution of a younger population among the Japanese as illustrated below in Table 6.

TABLE 6

AGE DISTRIBUTION OF CHINESE AND JAPANESE IN CALIFORNIA, 1910 CENSUS*

Age Periods	Chinese		Japanese		Total Population	
	Male	Female	Male	Female	Male	Female
Under 5 years..........	1.4	12.1	3.4	19.4	7.4	9.0
5– 9 years	1.3	12.3	1.2	6.2	6.7	8.3
10–14 years	2.3	10.6	0.5	2.1	6.6	8.2
15–19 years	6.5	8.0	4.2	3.8	7.7	8.9
20–24 years	6.6	10.6	16.0	16.7	9.9	9.8
25–34 years	11.8	18.4	45.5	37.6	20.7	18.8
35–44 years	17.5	14.3	22.3	12.0	16.3	15.1
45–64 years	44.2	12.1	5.4	1.8	18.7	16.7
65 and over............	4.6	1.4	0.1	...	5.4	5.1

* *United States Census Report, 1910*, Vol. II, p. 158.

Age groups of Chinese and Japanese.—The Chinese have the highest percentage in the age group 45–64 and over—44.2 for males and 12.1 for females; while the Japanese have the highest percentage in the age group 25–34 years—45.5 for males and 37.6 for females. The higher percentages among the Japanese are divided among the younger age groups, and, inversely, the higher percentages among the Chinese are divided among the older age groups.

An examination of the age grouping of the male and female Oriental population indicated the prevalence of family life, and explains the increase in the female population through the birth of female children. A relatively high percentage of the Chinese in the state is of the older and aging periods of life, while a larger percentage of the Japanese is composed of younger people and those approaching middle age, i.e., from 20 to 45. This, as remarked above, is due to changes in our immigration policy affecting the two races. With the cessation of Chinese immigration, those that did not return to China remained to settle and engage in divers occupations here. On the other hand, owing to somewhat different conditions, the Japanese, coming at a later period, bringing or sending for wives and brides, able to have family life, possess a larger proportion of young people now forming a second generation of Japanese in the country. The still more recent limitations placed upon Japanese entrance to the United States have had but a relatively brief period in which to influence the total situation.

Changes in Oriental geographical distribution in counties and cities.— It may be said that the Japanese "inherited" the localities first settled by the Chinese, for those counties and cities which have witnessed a decline in the number and percentage of Chinese population show a relatively high percentage of Japanese. The fluctuation in the Chinese and Japanese populations in the different localities in the state during the two decades, 1900–1920, is seen in Table 7.

TABLE 7

CHANGES IN NUMBER OF CHINESE AND JAPANESE POPULATION IN COUNTIES IN
CALIFORNIA, 1900, 1910, 1920*

County	In 1900		In 1910		In 1920	
	Chinese	Japanese	Chinese	Japanese	Chinese	Japanese
Alameda	2,211	1,149	4,588	3,266	4,505	5,221
Butte	712	365	572	295	289	423
Colusa	274	53	218	140	167	275
Contra Costa	627	276	550	1,009	343	846
Fresno	1,775	598	1,377	2,233	998	5,732
Kern	906	48	841	273	557	338
Kings	417	156	358	293	451	594
Los Angeles	3,209	204	2,602	8,461	2,591	19,911
Marin	489	52	555	199	252	140
Merced	357	43	278	98	135	420
Monterey	857	710	575	1,121	748	1,614
Napa	541	6	205	103	126	79
Nevada	632	15	309	22	120	16
Orange	136	3	83	641	26	1,491
Placer	1,050	133	612	862	419	1,474
Riverside	316	97	187	765	103	626
Sacramento	3,254	1,209	2,143	3,874	1,954	5,800
San Benito	69	15	66	286	104	427
San Bernardino	388	148	284	946	107	533
San Diego	414	25	430	520	307	1,431
San Francisco	13,954	1,781	10,582	4,518	7,744	5,358
San Joaquin	1,875	313	1,968	1,804	1,819	4,354
San Luis Obispo...........	154	16	165	434	77	501
San Mateo	306	46	309	358	342	663
Santa Barbara	459	114	440	863	341	930

* *United States Census Report, 1920,* Vol. III, Table 7, pp. 109–10.

TABLE 7—*Continued*

County	In 1900		In 1910		In 1920	
	Chinese	Japanese	Chinese	Japanese	Chinese	Japanese
Santa Clara	1,738	284	1,064	2,299	839	2,981
Santa Cruz	614	235	194	689	215	1,019
Solano	903	870	811	894	669	1,017
Sonoma	599	148	287	554	183	506
Sutter	226	155	79	134	42	373
Tulare	370	48	257	615	231	1,602
Ventura	408	94	235	872	155	675
Yolo	346	410	198	789	176	1,152
Yuba	719	56	493	336	359	355
Imperial	Not Incorporated		32	217	88	1,986

The changes in the volume of Chinese and Japanese population in the largest and most important cities in California are given below. To Los Angeles city have turned a greater number of Japanese, and in San Francisco have remained a larger proportion of the Chinese, alongside of whom have come the Japanese. In Sacramento and Fresno the Japanese have tended to replace the Chinese and in the other cities there have been similar changes.

TABLE 8

CHANGES IN THE NUMBER OF CHINESE AND JAPANESE POPULATION IN CITIES, 1900–1920*

City	In 1900		In 1910		In 1920	
	Chinese	Japanese	Chinese	Japanese	Chinese	Japanese
Alameda	255	110	217	499	94	644
Berkeley	154	17	451	710	337	911
Fresno	1,104	175	975	629	617	1,119
Los Angeles	2,111	150	1,954	4,238	2,062	11,618
Oakland	950	194	3,609	1,520	3,821	2,709
Pasadena	101	17	102	253	100	383
Sacramento	1,065	336	1,054	1,437	831	1,976
San Diego	292	14	348	159	254	772
San Francisco	13,954	1,781	10,582	4,518	7,744	5,358
San Jose	553	44	359	345	341	321
Stockton	593	39	698	475	1,071	840

* From *United States Census Report, 1920*, Vol. III.

The significance of the volume of the Oriental population is comprehended when it is seen what percentage they have formed of the total population in each locality at each census period.

TABLE 9

CHINESE AND JAPANESE PERCENTAGE OF TOTAL POPULATION IN CITIES,
1900, 1910, 1920*

City	In 1900			In 1910			In 1920		
	Popu-lation	Chi-nese	Japa-nese	Popu-lation	Chi-nese	Japa-nese	Popu-lation	Chi-nese	Japa-nese
Alameda	16,464	1.5	0.7	23,383	0.9	2.1	28,806	0.3	2.3
Berkeley	13,214	1.2	0.1	40,434	1.1	1.8	56,036	0.6	1.6
Fresno	12,470	8.9	1.4	24,892	3.9	2.5	45,086	1.4	2.5
Los Angeles	102,479	2.1	0.1	319,198	0.6	1.3	576,673	0.4	2.0
Oakland	66,960	1.4	0.3	150,174	2.4	1.0	216,261	1.8	1.3
Pasadena	9,117	1.1	0.2	30,291	0.3	0.8	45,354	0.2	0.8
Sacramento	29,282	3.6	1.1	44,696	2.4	3.2	65,908	1.3	3.0
San Diego	17,700	1.6	0.1	39,578	0.9	0.4	74,683	0.3	1.0
San Francisco	342,782	4.1	0.5	416,912	2.5	1.1	506,676	1.5	1.1
San Jose	21,500	2.6	0.2	28,946	1.2	1.2	39,642	0.9	0.8
Stockton	17,506	3.4	0.2	23,253	3.0	2.0	40,296	2.7	2.1

* From *United States Census Report, 1920*, Vol. III.

It is important to note that while the general population in each city steadily increased and the Chinese population considerably decreased, the Japanese population increased rapidly but seldom equaled the percentage of Chinese in 1900. Thus in 1900 the Chinese were 8.9 per cent of the population of Fresno, 4.1 per cent of the population of San Francisco, and 3.6 per cent of Sacramento. They decreased to 3.9 in 1910 in Fresno, to 2.5 per cent in San Francisco, and to 2.4 per cent in Sacramento. In 1920 the decline continued to 1.4 per cent in Fresno, 1.5 per cent in San Francisco, and 1.3 per cent in Sacramento. While the Japanese increased steadily in population in each center, yet the highest point they reached was to advance in Sacramento, from 1.1 per cent in 1900, to 3.2 per cent in 1910 and 3.0 per cent in 1920; in Fresno, from 1.4 per cent in 1900, to 2.5 per cent in 1910 and 1920; in Stockton, from 0.2 per cent in 1900, to 2.0 per cent in 1910 and 2.1 per cent in 1920. Otherwise the increase in these large cities brought them to the level of about 2.0 per cent of the total population.

In the counties the percentage they form of the total population is higher, for first the one then the other race came to certain parts of the countryside to engage in agriculture. In the early days the Chinese went to the mining counties, and sharp decreases in their numbers have since occurred.

Table 10 shows the changes in the percentages of the Chinese and Japanese population in the counties to which they came.

TABLE 10

CHINESE AND JAPANESE PERCENTAGE OF TOTAL POPULATION IN COUNTIES,
1900, 1910, 1920*

County	In 1900			In 1910			In 1920		
	Total in County	Percentage		Total in County	Percentage		Total in County	Percentage	
		Chinese	Japanese		Chinese	Japanese		Chinese	Japanese
Alameda	130,197	1.7	0.9	246,131	1.9	1.3	344,177	1.3	1.5
Butte	17,117	4.2	2.1	27,301	2.1	1.1	30,030	1.0	1.4
Colusa	7,364	3.7	0.7	7,732	2.8	1.8	9,290	1.8	3.0
Contra Costa	18,046	3.5	1.5	31,674	1.7	3.1	53,889	0.6	1.6
Fresno	37,862	4.7	1.6	75,657	1.8	3.0	128,779	0.8	4.5
Eldorado	8,986	2.3	0.3	7,492	0.8	0.4	6,426	0.3	0.7
Glenn	5,150	4.4	0.3	7,172	1.8	0.5	11,853	1.1	1.0
Imperial	Not Incorporated			13,591	0.2	1.5	43,453	0.2	4.6
Inyo	4,377	1.5	...	6,974	1.4	0.6	7,031	1.0	1.2
Kern	16,480	5.5	0.3	37,715	2.2	0.7	54,843	1.0	0.6
Kings	9,871	4.2	1.6	16,230	2.2	1.8	22,031	2.0	2.7
Lake	6,017	1.4	...	5,526	0.4	0.1	5,402	0.1	...
Lassen	4,511	0.6	...	4,802	0.3	0.1	8,507	0.8	0.1
Los Angeles	170,298	1.9	0.1	504,131	0.5	1.7	936,455	0.3	2.1
Madera	6,364	3.6	0.3	8,368	2.5	0.4	12,203	0.6	1.1
Marin	15,702	3.1	0.3	25,114	2.2	0.8	27,342	0.9	0.5
Mendocino	20,465	1.1	0.1	23,929	1.1	0.3	24,116	0.7	0.2
Merced	9,215	3.9	0.5	15,148	1.8	0.6	24,579	0.5	1.7
Monterey	19,380	4.4	3.7	24,146	2.4	4.6	27,980	2.7	5.8
Mono	2,167	5.6	...	2,042	1.0	0.7	960	0.5	0.2
Napa	16,451	3.3	...	19,800	1.0	0.5	20,678	0.6	0.4
Nevada	17,789	3.5	...	14,955	2.1	...	10,850	1.1	...
Orange	19,696	0.7	...	34,436	0.2	1.9	61,375	...	2.4
Placer	15,786	6.6	0.8	18,237	3.4	4.7	18,584	2.3	7.9
Plumas	4,657	4.1	...	5,259	2.0	0.4	5,681	1.3	0.4
Riverside	17,897	1.8	0.5	34,696	0.5	2.2	50,297	0.2	1.2
Sacramento	45,915	7.1	2.6	67,806	3.1	5.7	91,029	2.1	6.4
San Benito	6,633	1.0	0.2	8,041	0.8	3.6	8,995	1.2	4.7
San Bernardino	27,929	1.4	0.5	56,706	0.5	1.7	73,401	0.1	0.7
San Diego	35,090	1.2	0.1	61,665	0.7	0.8	112,248	0.3	1.3
San Francisco	342,782	3.4	0.4	416,912	2.5	1.1	506,676	1.5	1.1
San Joaquin	35,452	5.3	0.9	50,731	3.9	3.5	79,905	2.3	5.4
San Luis Obispo	16,637	0.9	0.1	19,383	0.9	2.2	21,893	0.4	2.3
San Mateo	12,094	2.5	0.4	26,585	1.2	1.3	36,781	0.9	1.8
Santa Barbara	18,934	2.4	0.6	27,738	1.6	3.1	41,097	0.8	2.3
Santa Clara	60,216	2.8	0.5	83,539	1.3	2.7	100,676	0.8	3.0
Santa Cruz	21,512	2.9	1.1	26,140	0.7	2.6	26,269	0.8	3.9
Shasta	17,318	0.6	0.1	18,920	0.5	0.2	13,361	0.2	...
Sierra	4,017	7.7	...	4,098	2.9	0.4	1,783	0.2	...
Siskiyou	16,962	4.7	...	18,801	1.8	0.1	18,545	0.7	...
Solano	24,143	3.7	3.6	27,559	2.9	3.2	40,602	1.6	2.5
Sonoma	38,480	1.6	0.4	48,394	0.6	1.1	52,090	0.4	1.0

* From *United States Census Report, 1920,* Vol. III, p. 109.

TABLE 10—*Continued*

County	In 1900			In 1910			In 1920		
	Total in County	Percentage		Total in County	Percentage		Total in County	Percentage	
		Chinese	Japanese		Chinese	Japanese		Chinese	Japanese
Sutter	5,886	3.8	2.6	6,328	1.2	2.1	10,115	0.4	3.7
Tehama	10,996	6.6	1.3	11,401	2.7	0.9	12,882	1.3	0.7
Trinity	4,383	7.7	...	3,301	4.9	...	2,551	2.0	...
Tulare	18,375	2.0	0.3	35,440	0.7	1.7	59,031	0.4	2.7
Ventura	14,367	2.8	0.7	18,347	1.3	4.8	28,724	0.5	2.3
Yolo	13,618	2.5	3.0	13,926	1.4	5.7	17,105	1.0	6.7
Yuba	8,620	8.3	0.6	10,042	4.9	3.3	10,375	3.5	3.4

At no time in any one county did either race come to constitute as high as 10 per cent of the total population.

The highest proportion that either race became of the total population of the localities in which they settled during the two-decade period was 8.3 per cent. And it must be remarked that in the counties in which they appear to be in largest number, such as in San Francisco, the percentage that they form of the total population is, throughout, comparatively low; for example, in Los Angeles, the percentage of the Chinese ranges from 1.9 in 1900 to 0.5 and 0.3, respectively, in 1910 and 1920; that of the Japanese ranges from 0.1 in 1900 to 1.7 in 1910 and to 2.1 in 1920. In San Francisco, the Chinese percentage ranges from 3.4 in 1900 to 2.5 in 1910, and to 1.5 in 1920; the Japanese from 0.4 in 1900 to 1.1 in 1910 and in 1920. These are the two most densely populated counties in the state, and their population is steadily increasing.

Principal Oriental settlements in California.—The cities in which Chinese and Japanese are domiciled in largest numbers at the present time (1920) are as shown in Table 11.

The largest populations of Orientals in cities are those in Los Angeles, San Francisco, Oakland, Sacramento, Stockton, Riverside, Alameda, Monterey, and San Jose.

The counties in which Orientals are now situated are as given in Table 12. It should be remembered, however, that there have been some changes in the distribution of the Oriental population since 1900. The relatively large numbers of Chinese in mining counties in 1900 have diminished by 1920, while city populations have increased, rural numbers tending to remain more nearly stable. The most noticeable change for the Japanese for the period is the tendency to move from some agricultural sections to the larger cities, due in part to adverse land legislation.

TABLE 11

NUMBER AND PERCENTAGE OF CHINESE AND JAPANESE IN CALIFORNIA CITIES, 1920

City	Total Population in City	Chinese		Japanese		Orientals	
		Number	Percentage	Number	Percentage	Number	Percentage
Alameda	28,806	94	0.3	644	2.2	738	2.6
Berkeley	56,036	337	0.6	911	1.6	1,248	2.2
Fresno	45,086	617	1.4	1,119	2.5	1,736	3.9
Los Angeles	576,673	2,062	0.4	11,618	2.0	13,680	2.4
Oakland	216,261	3,821	1.8	2,709	1.3	6,530	3.0
Sacramento	65,908	831	1.3	1,976	3.0	2,807	4.3
San Diego	74,683	254	0.3	772	1.0	1,026	1.4
San Jose	39,642	341	0.9	321	0.8	662	1.7
San Francisco	506,676	7,744	1.5	5,358	1.1	13,102	2.6
Stockton	40,296	1,071	2.7	840	2.1	1,911	4.7
Bakersfield	18,638	...	...	...	...	540	2.9
Marysville	5,461	...	...	...	...	502	9.2
Monterey	5,479	...	...	...	...	656	12.0
Pasadena	45,354	...	...	...	...	498	1.1
Riverside	19,341	...	...	...	...	1,393	7.2
Salinas	4,308	...	...	...	...	350	8.1
Santa Barbara	19,441	...	...	...	...	399	2.1
Vallejo	21,107	...	...	...	...	556	2.6
Watsonville	5,013	...	...	...	...	414	8.3

TABLE 12

NUMBER AND PERCENTAGE OF CHINESE AND JAPANESE IN CALIFORNIA COUNTIES, 1920

County	Total Population	Chinese		Japanese		Orientals	
		Number	Percentage	Number	Percentage	Number	Percentage
Alameda	344,177	4,505	1.3	5,221	1.5	9,726	2.8
Butte	30,030	289	1.0	423	1.4	714	2.4
Contra Costa	53,889	343	0.6	846	1.6	1,189	2.2
Fresno	128,779	998	0.8	5,732	4.5	6,730	5.3
Glenn	11,853	130	1.1	122	1.0	252	2.1
Imperial	43,453	88	0.2	1,986	4.6	2,074	4.8
Kern	54,843	557	1.0	338	0.6	895	1.6
Kings	22,031	451	2.0	594	2.7	1,045	4.7
Los Angeles	936,455	2,591	0.3	19,911	2.1	22,502	2.4
Marin	27,342	252	0.9	140	0.5	392	1.4
Merced	24,579	135	0.5	420	1.7	555	2.2
Monterey	27,980	748	2.7	1,614	5.8	2,362	8.5
Orange	61,375	26	...	1,491	2.4	1,517	2.4
Placer	18,584	419	2.3	1,474	7.9	1,893	10.2
Riverside	50,297	103	0.2	626	1.2	729	1.4

TABLE 12—*Continued*

County	Total Population	Chinese		Japanese		Orientals	
		Number	Percentage	Number	Percentage	Number	Percentage
Sacramento	91,029	1,954	2.1	5,800	6.4	7,754	8.5
San Benito	8,995	104	1.2	427	4.7	531	5.9
San Bernardino	73,401	107	0.1	533	0.7	640	0.8
San Diego	112,248	307	0.3	1,431	1.3	1,738	1.6
San Francisco	506,676	7,744	1.5	5,358	1.1	13,102	2.6
San Joaquin	79,905	1,819	2.3	4,354	5.4	6,173	7.7
San Luis Obispo	21,893	77	0.4	501	2.3	578	2.7
San Mateo	36,781	342	0.9	663	1.8	1,005	2.7
Santa Barbara	41,097	341	0.8	930	2.3	1,271	3.1
Santa Clara	100,676	839	0.8	2,981	3.0	3,820	3.8
Santa Cruz	26,269	215	0.8	1,019	3.9	1,234	4.7
Solano	40,602	669	1.6	1,017	2.5	1,686	4.1
Sonoma	52,090	183	0.4	506	1.0	689	1.4
Stanislaus	43,557	87	0.2	478	1.1	565	1.3
Sutter	10,115	42	0.4	373	3.7	415	4.1
Ventura	28,724	155	0.5	675	2.3	830	2.8
Tulare	59,031	231	0.4	1,602	2.7	1,833	3.1
Yolo	17,105	175	1.0	1,152	6.7	1,327	7.7
Yuba	10,375	359	8.5	355	3.4	714	6.9

The counties most heavily populated by Orientals are: Los Angeles, San Francisco, Fresno, San Joaquin, Alameda, Sacramento, Santa Clara, Monterey, Placer, San Diego, Imperial, Kings, Tulare, Ventura, and Yolo.

III. CHINESE AND JAPANESE ARRESTS IN CALIFORNIA

The Chinese and Japanese had settled and are now dispersed in community knots throughout the state. First the one then the other race settled in considerable numbers in certain localities, which they selected for economic reasons. It was thought that in beginning the examination of their delinquency with the year 1900 the full activities of both races for a representative period would be fairly covered. Another reason for the choice of this date is that it is doubtful whether any accurate or full records are available prior to that year. Accordingly, requests were made from city, county, and state police authorities to furnish, if possible, detailed records on Oriental delinquents. In addition, one or more research assistants were granted free access to the records in all the larger centers.

A large amount of information was obtained; but, owing to differences in police record-keeping, this information does not cover quite the same period of years in all cases. Thus, from eight centers records were obtained of arrests made between 1900 and 1927; from ten centers, records of arrests made between 1914 and 1927; from two centers records covering the period 1917–1927; from one center records covering the period 1918–1928, one center covering the period 1921–1927, one covering the period 1924–1926, and one covering the period 1925–1927. These differences are not serious enough to invalidate results. The information thus collected was organized and wherever advisable was thrown into tabular form. The more important of these tables are quoted in the study.

It will aid in the reading of this chapter, it may be suggested, if it be noted that in the early part of the chapter the record usually gives absolute numbers without making comparison with total population figures, but that comparison of this sort is made in the latter part of the chapter.

DISTRIBUTION OF ARRESTS OF ORIENTALS

Records of arrests of Orientals were assembled from the following centers: 9 cities, among which are included the largest cities in California, and in which Chinese and Japanese are the most densely settled; and 17 counties in which these races have been and are now domiciled in large numbers. The 26 centers listed below thus represent 80 per cent of the general population in the state and 89 per cent of the total Oriental population in the state.

TABLE 13

POPULATION OF CITIES AND COUNTIES REPORTING ON CHINESE
AND JAPANESE DELINQUENCY, 1920*

Locality	Total Population	Chinese	Japanese	Total Orientals
Cities				
Alameda	28,806	94	644	738
Berkeley	56,036	337	911	1,248
Los Angeles	576,673	2,062	11,618	13,680
Sacramento	65,908	831	1,976	2,807
San Francisco	506,676	7,744	5,358	13,102
Oakland	216,261	3,821	2,709	6,530
Stockton	40,296	1,071	840	1,911
San Jose	39,642	341	321	662
Santa Barbara	19,441	.....	.....	399
Counties				
Alameda	344,177	4,505	5,221	9,726
Fresno	128,779	998	5,732	6,730
Imperial	43,453	88	1,986	2,074
Kern	54,843	557	338	895
Kings	22,031	451	594	1,045
Marin	27,342	252	140	392
Monterey	27,980	748	1,614	2,362
Orange	61,375	26	1,491	1,517
Placer	18,584	419	1,474	1,893
Sacramento	91,029	1,954	5,800	7,754
San Benito	8,995	104	427	531
San Diego	112,248	307	1,431	1,738
San Joaquin	79,905	1,819	4,354	6,175
San Mateo	36,781	342	663	1,005
Santa Clara	100,676	839	2,981	3,820
Sutter	10,115	42	373	415
Nevada	10,850	309	22	331
Total	2,728,902	30,061	59,018	89,480

* *United States Census Report, 1920.*

VOLUME OF ARRESTS AND PENITENTIARY COMMITMENTS OF ORIENTALS

Records were obtained from twenty-five sources in the state, on 2,027,794 general arrests, covering stated periods between 1900 and 1927. Of these there were 88,927 Orientals; the Chinese arrested totaled 71,626 and the Japanese 17,727 (see Table 14).

The proportion which the Oriental arrests form of the total arrests in each locality is more clearly visualized in the table of percentages (Table 15). Thus out of over two million arrests, eighty-nine thousand were of Orientals, constituting 4.4 per cent of the total number. The Chinese ar-

TABLE 14

NUMBER OF CHINESE AND JAPANESE ARRESTS IN 25 CENTERS IN CALIFORNIA, 1900–1927

Period	Place	Total Arrests	Chinese	Japanese	Total Orientals
1900–27	San Quentin Prison...............	55,509	978	364	1,342
1900–27	Folsom Prison	10,410	50	18	68
1900–27	Alameda (city)	18,659	840	378	1,218
1900–27	Kings County	13,000*	400	235	635
1900–27	Orange County	15,000*	78	70	148
1900–27	San Diego County	29,435	1,060	479	1,539
1900–27	San Benito County	2,253	8	7	15
1900–27	Sutter County	1,814	7	12	19
1914–27	Los Angeles (city)...............	766,394	8,958	10,116	19,074
1914–27	Oakland (city)	260,289	2,806	1,362	4,168
1914–27	San Jose (city)	50,784	1,267	625	1,892
1914–27	Berkeley (city)	16,103	91	227	318
1914–27	Alameda County	12,605	144	46	190
1914–27	Kern County	12,634	319	20	339
1914–27	Fresno County	61,954	1,472	660	2,132
1914–27	Imperial County	13,689	275	272	547
1914–27	San Mateo County...............	12,593	129	18	147
1917–27	Santa Clara County..............	40,000*	394	51	445
1914–27	Monterey County	20,000*	111	21	132
1917–27	Sacramento County	14,124	832	168	1,000
1918–28	San Francisco (city).............	479,264	48,315	1,699	50,014
1918–27	Santa Barbara (city).............	15,000*	343	102	445
1921–27	Sacramento (city)	58,495	1,267	625	1,892
1924–26	San Joaquin County..............	19,464	476	29	505
1925–27	Stockton (city)	28,322	1,006	123	1,129
	Total	2,027,794	71,626	17,727	89,353

* Estimated.

rests form 3.5 per cent and the Japanese 0.9 per cent of the arrests made in the centers named in the table (p. 24).

The highest percentage the Orientals constitute of the entire number of arrests is in the city of San Francisco, where, in a relatively shorter period of time, Oriental arrests have come to form 10.4 per cent of the total for the city. In Sacramento County Oriental arrests constitute 7.1 per cent of the total, and in Stockton city and San Joaquin County they form 4.0 and 2.5 per cent, respectively. All of these are densely populated Oriental centers, and furnish numerous occasions for gambling, lottery, and narcotic raids.

Of all commitments to the penal institutions of the state during a period of 27 years, those of Orientals form 3.2 per cent. It should be remembered that such commitments are for heinous and primarily anti-social acts,

TABLE 15

PERCENTAGE OF CHINESE AND JAPANESE ARRESTS TO TOTAL ARRESTS IN
25 CENTERS IN CALIFORNIA

Period	Place	Number of Total Arrests	Percentage of Total Arrests in County and City		
			Chinese	Japanese	Orientals
1900–27	San Quentin Prison...............	55,509	1.8	0.7	2.5
1900–27	Folsom Prison....................	10,410	0.5	0.2	0.7
1900–27	Alameda (city)	18,659	4.5	2.0	6.5
1900–27	Kings County....................	13,000*	3.1	1.8	4.9
1900–27	Orange County...................	15,000*	0.5	0.5	1.0
1900–27	San Diego County................	29,435	3.6	1.6	5.2
1900–27	San Benito County...............	2,253	0.4	0.3	0.7
1900–27	Sutter County....................	1,814	0.4	0.7	1.1
1914–27	Los Angeles (city)...............	766,394	1.2	1.3	2.5
1914–27	Oakland (city)...................	260,289	1.1	0.5	1.6
1914–27	San Jose (city)..................	50,784	2.5	1.2	3.7
1914–27	Berkeley (city)..................	16,103	0.6	1.4	2.0
1914–27	Alameda County..................	12,605	1.1	0.4	1.5
1914–27	Kern County.....................	12,634	2.5	0.2	2.7
1914–27	Fresno County...................	61,954	2.4	1.1	3.5
1914–27	Imperial County.................	13,689	2.0	2.0	4.0
1914–27	San Mateo County...............	12,593	1.0	0.1	1.1
1914–27	Monterey County.................	20,000*	0.5	0.1	0.6
1917–27	Santa Clara County..............	40,000*	1.0	0.1	1.1
1917–27	Sacramento County..............	14,124	5.9	1.2	7.1
1918–27	Santa Barbara (city).............	15,000*	2.3	0.7	3.0
1918–28	San Francisco (city).............	479,264	10.1	0.3	10.4
1921–27	Sacramento (city)...............	58,495	2.2	1.1	3.3
1924–26	San Joaquin County..............	19,464	2.4	0.1	2.5
1925–27	Stockton (city)..................	28,322	3.6	0.4	4.0
1900–27	Marin County....................	10,000*	0.2	...	0.2
	Total	2,037,794	3.5	0.9	4.4

* Estimated.

inimical to good order, persons, and property. Of all those committed to San Quentin Prison, where prisoners are sent for life and long-term sentences, or awaiting execution, for all major crimes, the Orientals formed, for the entire period 1900–1927, 2.5 per cent (1.8 per cent Chinese and 0.7 per cent Japanese) for the entire state. At Folsom, to which are sent recidivists and especially difficult cases, the Orientals constituted 0.7 per cent of all prisoners committed during the period 1900–1927 from all over the state.

In the city of Los Angeles, where there is a large Oriental quarter, the Oriental arrests for a period of 13 years constituted 2.5 per cent of all arrests made in the city.

In the city of Oakland, where in 13 years 260,289 arrests were made, the Chinese formed 1.1 and the Japanese 0.5 per cent of the total.

In Fresno County, between 1914 and 1927, the Oriental arrests constituted 3.5 per cent—the Chinese arrests 2.4 per cent, and the Japanese 1.1 per cent. During the same period in Imperial County arrests of Orientals formed 4.0 per cent of the total, the Chinese being 2.0 and the Japanese 2.0 per cent. Both of these counties have considerable Oriental settlements.

Between 1900 and 1927 in San Diego County the Oriental arrests formed 5.2 per cent—the Chinese 3.6 per cent, and the Japanese 1.6 per cent. During the same period arrests of Orientals formed in Kings County 3.1 per cent for the Chinese and 1.8 per cent for the Japanese; in San Benito County, 0.4 per cent Chinese and 0.3 per cent Japanese; in Orange County, 1.0 per cent evenly divided between the two races; in Sutter County, 0.4 per cent for the Chinese and 0.7 per cent for the Japanese; and in the city of Alameda, 4.5 per cent for the Chinese and 2.0 per cent for the Japanese.

In the city of Sacramento, an important Oriental center, their arrests were 3.3 per cent of the total number made during the period 1921 to 1927 —2.2 per cent Chinese and 1.1 per cent Japanese.

From 1917 to 1927 in Santa Clara County the Oriental arrests are estimated to form 1.1 per cent of the total for the county; and for the same period in the city of Santa Barbara arrests of Orientals are estimated to constitute 3.0 per cent of the total.

In San Jose, the county seat of Santa Clara County, where the Oriental percentage of the total population is relatively large, such arrests form 3.7 per cent of the total number made between 1914 and 1927 in the city. During this period in the city of Berkeley they formed 2.0 per cent of the total; in Alameda County, 1.5 per cent; in Kern County, 2.7 per cent; in Monterey County, 0.6 per cent; and in San Mateo County, 1.1 per cent.

Progression of Oriental arrests.—Does the number of Orientals arrested increase or decrease in successive years? An examination of the records for each center shows that there is no tendency toward an increase but that in most centers the proportion of Orientals arrested has declined, and that where there is no decrease the volume has remained almost stationary, there being a slight increase in only one center. It is safe to draw from this the inference that with time there has come adaptability to our laws and repression of recurring criminal practices.

The best evidence of this fact is from the statistics for San Quentin prison, which indicate criminal conditions of the entire state. In the table (p. 26) it is seen that, whereas in 1900 Orientals in San Quentin formed 4.7 per cent of the prisoners committed during that year, in 1927 they con-

TABLE 16

NUMBER OF CHINESE AND JAPANESE PRISONERS AND THEIR PERCENTAGE OF TOTAL
PRISONERS AT SAN QUENTIN PRISON, 1900–1927

Year	Total Number Committed	Number of Orientals Committed			Percentage of Orientals Committed		
		Chinese	Japanese	Total	Chinese	Japanese	Total
1900–1901	1,309	58	4	62	4.4	0.3	4.7
1901–1902	1,476	54	7	61	3.7	0.5	4.2
1902–1903	1,529	55	11	66	3.6	0.7	4.3
1903–1904	1,476	55	11	66	3.7	0.7	4.4
1904–1905	1,588	49	7	56	3.1	0.4	3.5
1905–1906	1,588	50	6	56	3.1	0.4	3.5
1906–1907	1,549	42	10	52	2.7	0.6	3.3
1907–1908	1,702	36	14	50	2.1	0.8	2.9
1908–1909	1,814	33	15	48	1.8	0.8	2.6
1909–1910	1,922	22	16	38	1.1	0.8	1.9
1910–1911	1,881	23	18	41	1.2	1.0	2.2
1911–1912	1,937	16	24	40	0.8	1.2	2.0
1912–1913	1,929	11	15	26	0.6	0.8	1.4
1913–1914	2,209	22	19	41	1.0	0.9	1.9
1914–1915	2,312	22	23	45	1.0	1.0	2.0
1915–1916	2,308	2	6	8	0.1	0.3	0.4
1916–1917	2,160	9	4	13	0.4	0.2	0.6
1917–1918	1,930	19	5	24	1.0	0.3	1.3
1918–1919	1,817	31	12	43	1.7	0.7	2.4
1919–1920	1,848	33	2	35	1.8	0.1	1.9
1920–1921	2,030	36	16	52	1.8	0.8	2.6
1921–1922	2,445	58	20	78	2.4	0.8	3.2
1922–1923	2,391	57	27	84	2.4	1.1	3.5
1923–1924	2,647	49	22	71	1.9	0.8	2.7
1924–1925	2,903	46	19	65	1.6	0.6	2.2
1925–1926	3,280	46	17	63	1.4	0.5	1.9
1926–1927	3,529	44	14	58	1.2	0.4	1.6
Total	55,509	978	364	1,342	1.76	0.65	2.4

stituted but 1.6 per cent of the prisoners committed in that year. This
decrease from 1900 continued steadily until 1915 and 1916; at these dates
Oriental prisoners constituted only 0.4 and 0.6 per cent of the total prison
group which had at the same time been rising and which comprised the
largest number of commitments up to that time. The largest number of
Oriental commitments was in 1922, totaling 84, and forming 3.5 per cent
of the total in the prison. And while the general number increased after
that date, the Oriental number decreased. Thus it is clear that the highest
proportion of commitments was during the opening years of this century;
and it should be added that the Chinese comprise the major portion of
Oriental offenders throughout the period reviewed. The analysis of the

nature of offenses committed by them, which appears further on, may explain this difference.

The general number of commitments to San Quentin increased steadily from 1,309 in 1900–1901 to 3,529 in 1926–1927. The number of Chinese commitments decreased from 58 to 44, and in no year were there more than 58. The Japanese form a considerably smaller number and proportion of the commitments; the smallest number committed was 4 in 1900, and the largest number 27 in 1922. In 1926–1927 occurred the largest number of commitments for the entire quarter-century, and among these the Chinese numbered 44 and the Japanese 14, forming 1.2 and 0.4 per cent, respectively, of the entire number of commitments for the state. This is for the Japanese a slightly higher number than at the beginning of the century but lower than in many of the intervening years, and for the Chinese a number lower than for 1900–1901 and also lower than for about half the intervening years.

San Francisco's Chinatown is almost universally known. And mixed are the general feelings and expectations regarding the life that goes on there, so strange to Occidental eyes. The Chinese and Japanese who now live there are engaged mostly in mercantile pursuits, and the data that follow reflect a permanent and not transitory population.

The outstanding feature of this situation is that the proportion of Oriental arrests to total arrests in the city for the period of almost a complete decade decreased from 20.6 per cent in 1918, to 8.05 per cent in

TABLE 17

NUMBER AND PERCENTAGE OF CHINESE AND JAPANESE ARRESTED IN
SAN FRANCISCO, 1918 TO 1927–1928

Year	Total Number of Arrests	Number of Orientals			Percentage of Orientals		
		Chinese	Japanese	Total	Chinese	Japanese	Total
1918	23,061	4,568	181	4,749	19.8	0.8	20.6
1919	49,647	6,108	148	6,256	12.3	0.4	12.7
1920	26,673	3,907	132	4,039	14.6	0.5	15.1
1921	30,106	5,282	172	⋅5,454	17.5	0.6	18.1
1922	39,888	4,546	164	4,710	11.4	0.4	11.6
1923	40,633	2,808	84	2,892	6.9	0.2	7.1
1924	42,082	3,429	76	3,505	8.1	0.2	8.3
1925	46,180	3,990	267	4,257	8.6	0.6	9.2
1926	59,450	3,641	178	3,819	6.1	0.3	6.4
1927	60,772	4,358	205	4,563	7.2	0.3	7.5
1927–1928	60,772*	4,790	92	4,882	7.9	0.15	8.05
Total	479,264	47,427	1,699	49,126	9.9	0.4	10.3

* Estimated.

1928, a difference of 12.5 per cent, and that the decline in proportion went on rather steadily year by year, for both races: the Chinese percentage decreased from 19.8 in 1918 to 7.9 in 1928, and the Japanese from 0.8 in 1918 to 0.15 in 1928.

While the total number of arrests in the city increased quite considerably in volume, the volume of Chinese arrests did not increase in proportion but maintained a level which, beside the general increase, brought the percentage of their arrests lower and lower each year. The number of Japanese arrests decreased from 181 in 1918 to 92 in 1928, and only in two years did they exceed the 1918 number: 267 in 1925 and 205 in 1927. The highest number of arrests for the Chinese occurred in 1919, when they totaled 6,108, and the lowest number was in 1923, when they were 2,808; during this same period the total arrests being made in the city increased from 23,061 in 1918 to 60,772 in 1927–1928, an increase of 62.6 per cent. The lowest number of general arrests occurred in 1918 and the highest number in 1927–1928.

It may be repeated that since the data above run for the period 1918 to 1927–1928, they reflect a period when there were no marked changes in the size or the personnel of the Oriental population; on the contrary, it may be accepted that both of these have remained practically constant. This being so, the police records reviewed here bespeak a steadily increasing obedience to our laws and, inversely, a decrease in any tendency for the Oriental sections to become crime centers.

Los Angeles.—The city of Los Angeles, the largest city in California, and the metropolis of the southern part of the state, has an Oriental quarter which exceeds in numbers that of San Francisco; in the city of Los Angeles in 1920 there were 13,680 Orientals and in San Francisco there were 13,102. But the distribution of the two races is transposed in the two cities: Los Angeles exceeded San Francisco in the number of Japanese domiciled there, having 11,618 to 5,358 in San Francisco; and in San Francisco there were 7,744 Chinese to 2,062 in Los Angeles. This circumstance may largely explain the difference in the number of Japanese arrests in the two centers.

With regard to the progress of Oriental arrests, it is to be noted that for both races the proportion of their arrests to the general arrests in the city did not increase with the time but either remained constant or, in a few instances, decreased.

From 1914 to 1927 the total general arrests in the city ranged from 34,738 in 1922 to 85,225 in 1921, and averaged 54,764. During this period the Chinese arrests ranged from 306 in 1915 to 1,146 in 1927, averaging 642; and the Japanese ranged from 312 in 1921 to 1,295 in 1919, and averaged 723, but each averaged about the same proportion to the general

TABLE 18

NUMBER AND PERCENTAGE OF CHINESE AND JAPANESE ARRESTED IN
LOS ANGELES (CITY), 1914–1927

Year	Total Number of Arrests	Number of Orientals			Percentage of Orientals		
		Chinese	Japanese	Total	Chinese	Japanese	Total
1914	40,200	477	624	1,101	1.2	1.6	2.8
1915	41,414	306	431	737	0.7	1.0	1.7
1916	41,414	721	771	1,492	1.7	1.9	3.6
1917	49,136	483	781	1,264	1.0	1.6	2.6
1918	44,205	570	1,033	1,603	1.3	2.3	3.6
1919	47,637	839	1,295	2,133	1.8	2.7	4.5
1920	77,356	516	997	1,513	0.67	1.3	1.97
1921	85,225	491	312	803	0.57	0.37	0.94
1922	34,738	412	377	789	1.2	1.1	2.3
1923	47,729	584	412	996	1.2	0.87	2.07
1924	48,592	816	576	1,392	1.7	1.2	2.9
1925	58,416	1,040	754	1,794	1.8	1.3	3.1
1926	69,089	588	620	1,208	0.9	0.9	1.8
1927	81,243	1,146	1,133	2,279	1.4	1.4	2.8
Total	766,394	8,988	10,116	19,104	1.2	1.3	2.5

arrests in the city. The Japanese have a slightly larger volume of arrests (10,116) than the Chinese (8,988) for the total period; and each year except from 1921 to 1925 the Japanese have a somewhat larger number also.

In 1921 occurred the largest number of arrests, 85,225, in the city, and precisely in this year the Japanese had the lowest number and the Chinese the second lowest number of arrests made from among them at any one year before or after this date. In this year also, therefore, occurred the lowest proportion to the total number of arrests that they formed during the entire 13-year period: the Chinese, 0.57 per cent and the Japanese, 0.37 per cent. In no one year did the Chinese arrests amount to more than 1.8 per cent of the total city arrests; and the highest point for the Japanese was 2.7 per cent.

Oakland.—Oakland is the third largest city in California; it is third also in the relative size of its Oriental population. In Oakland there are about 6,500 Orientals, 3,800 of whom are Chinese. The Oakland data corresponding to those just given for Los Angeles, are shown in Table 19 (p. 30).

The volume of Chinese arrests is larger than that of the Japanese, there being 2,806 of the former and 1,362 of the latter during the period 1914–1927. The number of arrests of Chinese ranged from 121 in 1916 to 390 in 1920, and averaged 200. Among the Japanese, arrests ranged

TABLE 19

NUMBER AND PERCENTAGE OF CHINESE AND JAPANESE ARRESTED IN
OAKLAND, CALIFORNIA, 1914–1927

Year	Total Number of Arrests	Number of Orientals			Percentage of Orientals		
		Chinese	Japanese	Total	Chinese	Japanese	Total
1914	13,545	185	69	254	1.4	0.5	1.9
1915	17,310	274	63	337	1.6	0.4	2.0
1916	18,592	121	78	199	0.6	0.4	1.0
1917	19,030	145	58	203	0.8	0.3	1.1
1918	18,469	123	57	180	0.7	0.3	1.0
1919	21,110	258	54	312	1.2	0.3	1.5
1920	19,870	390	128	518	2.0	0.6	2.6
1921	19,640	270	156	426	1.4	0.8	2.2
1922	20,460	226	214	440	1.1	1.0	2.1
1923	20,340	192	166	358	0.9	0.8	1.7
1924	19,570	145	124	269	0.7	0.6	1.3
1925	17,451	125	64	189	0.7	0.4	1.1
1926	16,938	141	50	191	0.8	0.3	1.1
1927	17,964	211	81	292	1.2	0.5	1.7
Total	260,289	2,806	1,362	4,168	1.07	0.5	1.6

from 50 in 1926 to 214 in 1922, and averaged 97. Among the Chinese there seems to be maintained a more nearly uniform level, the proportion of their arrests to total arrests varying between 0.6 and 2.0 per cent, and without any tendency to violent upward changes. Among the Japanese, arrests to total arrests in the city have remained 1 per cent or less throughout, reaching 1 per cent only in one year, 1922, and thereafter gradually assuming and maintaining a downward trend.

Sacramento.—Sacramento is not only the capital city for the state, but also the county seat of Sacramento County, which is one of the most important Oriental counties in the state. The city itself has almost three thousand Orientals, two-thirds of whom are Japanese. The record for Sacramento is shown in Table 20.

While there is a general and appreciable increase in the total number of arrests in the city from 1921 to 1927, there is a quite steady decrease in the number of arrests among both Chinese and Japanese during the same period. The proportion of their arrests to total arrests shows a considerable net decrease: from 2.8 per cent in 1921 to 1.0 per cent in 1927 for the Chinese, and from 1.9 per cent in 1921 to 0.9 per cent in 1927 for the Japanese, or a decrease from 4.7 to 1.9 per cent for total Oriental arrests in a period of seven years. In 1923 there occurred the largest number of arrests in the city, 10,357, and among these, the Chinese ac-

TABLE 20

NUMBER AND PERCENTAGE OF CHINESE AND JAPANESE ARRESTED IN
SACRAMENTO (CITY), CALIFORNIA, 1921–1927

Year	Total Number of Arrests	Number of Orientals			Percentage of Orientals		
		Chinese	Japanese	Total	Chinese	Japanese	Total
1921	6,641	184	129	313	2.8	1.9	4.7
1922	6,210	113	73	186	1.8	1.2	3.0
1923	10,357	182	45	227	1.8	0.4	2.2
1924	8,930	133	42	175	1.5	0.5	2.0
1925	7,371	174	47	221	2.4	0.6	3.0
1926	9,093	85	54	139	0.9	0.6	1.5
1927	9,893	100	83	183	1.0	0.9	1.9
Total	58,495	971	473	1,444	1.7	0.8	2.5

counted for 182 and the Japanese for 45. In the last year, 1927, there were
almost ten thousand arrests in the city, over three thousand more than
in 1921, and in the same year, the Chinese arrests were 100, being less
than they were in 1921 by 84. The Japanese in 1927 had 83 arrests, 46
less than in 1921.

San Jose.—A similar tabulation for San Jose is given below:

TABLE 21

NUMBER AND PERCENTAGE OF CHINESE AND JAPANESE ARRESTED IN
SAN JOSE, CALIFORNIA, 1914–1927

Year	Total Number of Arrests	Number of Orientals			Percentage of Orientals		
		Chinese	Japanese	Total	Chinese	Japanese	Total
1914	2,396	50	13	63	2.1	0.5	2.6
1915	2,019	57	22	79	2.8	1.1	3.9
1916	2,140	75	25	100	3.5	1.2	4.7
1917	2,333	92	34	126	3.9	1.5	5.4
1918	1,650	60	51	111	3.6	3.1	6.7
1919	1,268	40	16	56	3.2	1.3	4.5
1920	2,055	38	28	66	1.8	1.4	3.2
1921	2,681	60	23	83	2.2	0.9	3.1
1922	4,091	59	37	96	1.4	0.9	2.3
1923	5,572	539	77	616	9.7	1.4	11.1
1924	5,522	61	58	119	1.1	1.0	2.1
1925	6,100	50	50	100	0.8	0.8	1.6
1926	6,229	27	95	122	0.4	1.5	1.9
1927	6,728	59	96	155	0.9	1.4	2.3
Total	50,784	1,267	625	1,892	2.5	1.2	3.7

In 1923 the San Jose Police Department executed a large number of lottery raids, and arrests for this misdemeanor swelled the volume of Chinese apprehensions. Yet, with the exception of the sudden rise in 1923, the proportion of the Chinese arrests to total city arrests shows a tendency to decrease. Japanese arrests show, on the whole, an increase. The highest point for the Japanese is 3.1 per cent, in 1918; the lowest 0.5 per cent, in 1914; and throughout they run usually a fraction over 1 per cent.

Stockton.—Stockton is the county seat of San Joaquin County, an important Oriental center, and itself possesses an appreciable Oriental population, the Chinese exceeding the Japanese.

It was not possible to obtain police records for more than the three years 1925 to 1927, and the table below reflects conditions then current.

TABLE 22

NUMBER AND PERCENTAGE OF CHINESE AND JAPANESE ARRESTED IN STOCKTON, CALIFORNIA, 1925–1927

Year	Total Number of Arrests	Number of Orientals			Percentage of Orientals		
		Chinese	Japanese	Total	Chinese	Japanese	Total
1925	9,162	200	44	244	2.2	0.5	2.7
1926	8,805	581	64	645	6.6	0.7	7.3
1927	10,355	225	15	240	2.2	0.1	2.3
Total	28,322	1,006	123	1,129	3.6	0.4	4.0

It seems possible that, as in the case of the sudden rise in the volume of Chinese arrests in the city of San Jose, the marked increase in 1926 in Stockton is due also to special raids.

Sacramento County.—The county of Sacramento is one of the centers in which both the Chinese and the Japanese settled in large numbers, and in which is at present contained an important proportion of the Oriental population of the state. Formerly the Chinese predominated, but at present the Japanese are about three times as numerous as the Chinese, and their chief occupation is agriculture. Arrests in the county were as shown in Table 23 on the opposite page.

With the exception of 1922, which appears to be perhaps a year devoted to "raiding activities" in the Oriental quarter, the Oriental arrests do not assume any remarkable proportion or tendency. On the whole (excepting the percentage 36.8 of Oriental arrests in 1922, which seems abnormal), there is a slight but definite downward movement, in both numbers and percentage.

TABLE 23

NUMBER AND PERCENTAGE OF CHINESE AND JAPANESE ARRESTED IN
SACRAMENTO COUNTY, 1917–1927

Year	Total Number of Arrests	Number of Orientals			Percentage of Orientals		
		Chinese	Japanese	Total	Chinese	Japanese	Total
1917	1,005	63	10	73	6.3	1.0	7.3
1918	744	18	11	29	2.4	1.5	3.9
1919	1,180	86	17	103	7.3	1.4	8.7
1920	1,027	90	6	96	8.8	0.6	9.4
1921	1,224	58	18	76	4.7	1.5	6.2
1922	337	111	13	124	32.9	3.9	36.8
1923	1,808	125	11	136	6.9	0.6	7.5
1924	1,771	138	15	153	7.8	0.8	8.6
1925	1,595	43	33	76	2.7	2.1	4.8
1926	1,661	41	6	47	2.5	0.4	2.9
1927	1,772	59	28	87	3.3	1.6	4.9
Total	14,124	832	168	1,000	5.9	1.2	7.1

Fresno County.—Fresno County ranks with Sacramento County in its importance as an Oriental agricultural center and as one in which both races have been and still are significantly represented.

TABLE 24

NUMBER AND PERCENTAGE OF CHINESE AND JAPANESE ARRESTED IN
FRESNO COUNTY, 1914–1927

Year	Total Number of Arrests	Number of Orientals			Percentage of Orientals		
		Chinese	Japanese	Total	Chinese	Japanese	Total
1914	5,320	44	15	59	0.8	0.3	1.1
1915	5,470	112	30	142	2.0	0.5	2.5
1916	5,037	140	55	195	2.8	1.1	3.9
1917	5,192	177	100	277	3.4	1.9	5.3
1918	5,762	59	29	88	1.0	0.5	1.5
1919	3,969	88	30	118	2.2	0.8	3.0
1920	3,015	47	31	78	1.6	1.0	2.6
1921	4,603	76	28	104	1.7	0.6	2.3
1922	3,917	90	48	138	2.3	1.2	3.5
1923	4,359	36	57	93	0.8	1.3	2.1
1924	4,242	131	66	197	3.1	1.6	4.7
1925	3,780	331	73	404	8.8	1.9	10.7
1926	3,652	86	72	158	2.4	2.0	4.4
1927	3,636	55	26	81	1.5	0.7	2.2
Total	61,954	1,472	660	2,132	2.4	1.1	3.5

The volume of Oriental arrests in this county seems to have moved with the volume of general county arrests, with two exceptions: in 1925 the volume of county arrests dropped and Oriental arrests, notably the Chinese, rose quite considerably; and in 1917 another quite perceptible rise in Oriental arrests occurred, when the Chinese arrests were 177 as compared to 44 in 1914, and the Japanese arrests rose to 100, as compared to 15 in 1914.

Imperial County.—Imperial County has only recently become an important Oriental center, having been settled primarily by the Japanese for agricultural purposes.

TABLE 25

NUMBER AND PERCENTAGE OF CHINESE AND JAPANESE ARRESTED IN
IMPERIAL COUNTY, 1914–1927

Year	Total Number of Arrests	Number of Orientals			Percentage of Orientals		
		Chinese	Japanese	Total	Chinese	Japanese	Total
1914	805	11	1	12	1.4	0.1	1.5
1915	576	19	4	23	3.3	0.7	4.0
1916	503	2	1	3	0.4	0.2	0.6
1917	748	5	2	7	0.7	0.3	1.0
1918	2,452	1	8	9	0.0	0.3	0.3
1919	580	9	36	45	1.6	6.2	7.8
1920	762	23	15	38	3.0	2.0	5.0
1921	781	106	16	122	13.6	2.0	15.6
1922	756	7	15	22	0.9	2.0	2.9
1923	999	3	33	36	0.3	3.3	3.6
1924	1,538	11	29	40	0.7	1.9	2.6
1925	1,580	7	25	32	0.4	1.6	2.0
1926	1,683	30	21	51	1.8	1.2	3.0
1927	2,106	41	66	107	1.9	3.1	5.0
Total	15,869	275	272	547	1.7	1.7	3.4

It is evident that arrests of Orientals constitute here a small part of the total number arrested every year. There is, however, the marked exception of 1921, when out of a total of 781 there were 106 Chinese arrests, due, as will be seen later, to their efforts at smuggling in aliens. In concert with the movement of general city arrests, there is an increase in the number of Japanese arrested. It is of interest that the highest number of arrests in the city was in 1918, when there were 2,452 apprehensions by the county police, and that among these were included only one Chinese and eight Japanese. With the exception of the relatively very high number of Chinese arrested in 1921, there is a fairly sustained level during the other years, not exceeding 41 in 1927. It should be noted that 1927 is the year when the highest volume of arrests since 1918 was reached. And while the general arrests in the county rose from 805 in 1914 to 2,106 in 1927, the Japanese arrests did not that year exceed 66, which is the highest number of arrests for them during the entire period. The proportion of their arrests to the volume of county arrests fell from 6.2 per cent in 1919 to 3.1 per cent in 1927, forming as low a proportion also as 1.2 per cent in 1926; while from 1914 to 1918, their proportion of arrests constituted even less than 1 per cent. The proportion of the Chinese arrests wavered between almost 0.0 per cent and 3.0 per cent, and shows no tendency toward an upward movement.

Alameda County.—Alameda County usually has contained a numerous Chinese and Japanese population. Considering that there are domiciled there about 4,500 Chinese and 5,500 Japanese, the following record pertaining to arrests is interesting.

TABLE 26

NUMBER AND PERCENTAGE OF CHINESE AND JAPANESE ARRESTED IN
ALAMEDA COUNTY, 1914–1927

Year	Total Number of Arrests	Number of Orientals			Percentage of Orientals		
		Chinese	Japanese	Total	Chinese	Japanese	Total
1914	630	21	0	21	3.3	0.0	3.3
1915	710	27	5	32	3.8	0.7	4.5
1916	530	5	3	8	0.9	0.6	1.5
1917	899	18	6	24	2.0	0.7	2.7
1918	850	2	3	5	0.2	0.4	0.6
1919	940	1	2	3	0.1	0.2	0.3
1920	1,030	2	2	4	0.2	0.2	0.4
1921	1,186	5	1	6	0.4	0.1	0.5
1922	1,194	4	4	8	0.3	0.3	0.6
1923	1,210	0	4	4	0.0	0.3	0.3
1924	960	19	8	27	2.0	0.8	2.8
1925	795	24	1	25	3.0	0.1	3.1
1926	800	10	0	10	1.2	0.0	1.2
1927	871	6	7	13	0.7	0.8	1.5
Total	12,605	144	46	190	1.1	0.4	1.5

General county arrests have risen, and in one group of years running from 1920 to 1923 rather higher than in any preceding or following period. Yet during the period 1918 to 1923, when total county arrests rose from 850 to 1,210, Oriental arrests did not exceed 8, and the highest number of Chinese arrests during this time was 5, and of the Japanese 4, and the proportion of their arrests in this six-year period did not for either race exceed 0.6 per cent. In 1923, the year when the largest number of arrests were made in the county (1,210), no Chinese were arrested and only 4 Japanese. And throughout the entire fourteen-year period the Chinese arrests did not, in any one year, exceed 27, and the highest number for the Japanese was 8.

Percentage of Oriental Arrests to Total Population

Pursuing the question as to what proportion the Oriental arrests form of the total arrests made in each center and in the state, we may ask what proportion of the population they constitute? The answer to the former question gives the place of the Oriental among the arrested population: this, for the twenty-five centers in the state for which there are data, is seen to be 4.4 per cent of the total.[1] We now proceed to consider what ratio of the population the arrested Orientals form.

San Quentin Prison.—Because of the small number of Orientals committed it is not possible to calculate separately for each year, but we may make a general statement for the whole period.

The total population in the state as shown by the largest pertinent census (1920) was 3,426,681. The number of Orientals committed to San Quentin from 1900 to 1927 was 1,342 (Table 14), which forms 0.04 of the total (1920) population. In other words, during a period of 27 years, the Orientals convicted and committed to the penitentiary for serious crimes constitute one twenty-fifth of 1 per cent.

There is, however, another observation in this regard: The Chinese and Japanese together constituted (1920) 2.9 per cent (Table 1) of the total population of the state. And the Chinese and Japanese together form 2.4 per cent (deduced from Table 1) of the population accumulated at San Quentin during the past 27 years, upon which it may be remarked that the ratio of their criminal population is lower than that of their general population. For each group separately this does not hold: the ratio of the Chinese general population to total general population in the state in 1920 was 0.8 per cent; and the ratio of the Chinese population accumulated at San Quentin since 1900, was 1.76 per cent. The ratio of the Japanese general population to the total state population was 2.1 per cent in 1920; yet their prison population ratio was 0.65 per cent. From all this it may perhaps be deduced that the Japanese contribution to the criminal population of the state is less than one-third of what might be expected from their portion of the population and that of the Chinese more than double what might be expected. Further discussion of this point appears below.

---

[1] See Table 15, p. 24.

Another way of ascertaining what part of the total population in the state is formed by the Oriental criminals is to calculate their ratios for the three census periods separately. The population in the state in 1900 was 1,485,053; and from 1900 to 1910, there were 454 Chinese and 101 Japanese committed to San Quentin. The Chinese criminals thus constituted approximately 0.03 per cent of the total general population in the state, and the Japanese 0.007 per cent. Of the criminal population in San Quentin during this period, the Chinese formed 2.9 per cent and the Japanese 0.6 per cent. And of the general population, the total general Chinese population in the state formed 3.2 per cent and the Japanese 0.7 per cent. During the census period 1911 to 1919, there were committed to San Quentin 188 Chinese and 128 Japanese. The total population in the state had now become 2,377,549. The ratio of the number of Chinese criminals to the total population in the state became now 0.008, and that of the Japanese, 0.005. Of the criminal population at San Quentin during this decade, the Chinese formed 0.96 per cent and the Japanese 0.64 per cent. The ratio of the Chinese general population in the state at this census

TABLE 27

RATIO OF CHINESE AND JAPANESE PRISONERS IN SAN QUENTIN TO
GENERAL POPULATION IN STATE

Census Year	Population of State	Total Oriental Prisoners		Percentage of Total Population		Oriental Percentage of Total Prisoners		Oriental Percentage of Total Population	
		Chinese	Japanese	Chinese	Japanese	Chinese	Japanese	Chinese	Japanese
1900....	1,485,053	454	101	0.03	0.007	2.9	0.6	3.2	0.7
1910....	2,377,549	188	128	0.008	0.005	0.9	0.6	1.5	1.7
1920....	3,426,861	336	135	0.01	0.004	1.8	0.7	0.8	2.1

period was 1.5 per cent, and of the Japanese, 1.7 per cent. In 1920 the general population in the state had increased to 3,426,861. The convicted Chinese, for the period 1919–1927, numbered 336 and the Japanese 135. The ratio of Chinese prisoners to total population is for this period 0.01, and of the Japanese 0.004. Of the prison population for this period, the Chinese ratio is 1.8, and the Japanese 0.73. And the ratio of the Chinese general population to the total state population is in this census period 0.8 per cent, and the Japanese ratio 2.1 per cent. While it is true that the census population figures are for a single year and the arrest figures cover a series of years during which the population total is changing, nevertheless the error is bound to be slight because of the very small numbers of Orientals involved. This is illustrated in Table 27.

The number of Oriental criminals during each census period is so small that it is difficult to calculate its proportion in the total body of the population.

Folsom Prison.—For Folsom Prison a calculation of this nature cannot be made with regard to its Oriental population, since during the entire period, 1900 to 1927, there were in all but 68 Oriental commitments to that institution.

San Francisco (city).—The arrest records available for San Francisco begin with the year 1918; therefore two census periods are to be considered, 1910 and 1920.

In 1910 the Orientals formed 3.6 per cent of the entire population of the city, the Chinese constituting 2.5 per cent and the Japanese 1.1 per cent. In 1920 the Chinese formed 1.5 per cent and the Japanese 1.0 per cent, together 2.5 per cent, of the total city population.

The following table shows the proportion that the Oriental arrests formed of the total population in the city each year.

TABLE 28

PERCENTAGE OF CHINESE AND JAPANESE ARRESTED TO TOTAL POPULATION IN
SAN FRANCISCO (CITY), 1918–1928*

Year	Number of Orientals Arrested		Total Population	Percentage of Total Population	
	Chinese	Japanese		Chinese	Japanese
1918...................	4,568	181	416,912 (1910)	1.1	0.04
1919...................	6,108	148		1.5	0.03
1920...................	3,907	132	506,676 (1920)	0.8	0.03
1921...................	5,282	172		1.0	0.03
1922...................	4,546	164		0.9	0.03
1923...................	2,808	84		0.5	0.02
1924...................	3,429	76		0.7	0.01
1925...................	3,990	267		0.8	0.05
1926...................	3,641	178		0.7	0.04
1927...................	4,358	205		0.9	0.04
1928...................	4,790	92		0.9	0.02
Total................	47,427	1,699	....	0.9	0.03

* In computing percentages of Oriental arrests to total city and county population, in this and following tables, a certain inaccuracy is inevitable, since the census figures of population are taken for a single year, while the arrests change from year to year. Yet in dealing with such small percentage figures the inaccuracy is bound to be very slight.

The Chinese arrests formed, during the 1910 census period, close to 1.5 per cent of the total population in the city. At this time they were calculated to constitute 2.5 per cent of the general population. The Japanese number of arrests at this period was too slight to allow of such calculation. In the 1920 census the Chinese population ratio in the city dropped to 1.5 per cent. Their proportion of arrests to general population in the city reached the 0.8 per cent mark in 1920, and 0.9 per cent in 1922 and 1928, with the percentage grading down to 0.5 in 1923. The average percentage for the entire period is 0.9. The average for the Japanese for the entire period is 0.03 per cent.

Los Angeles (*city*).—In 1910 the population of the city of Los Angeles is given in the census as 319,198; of this total the Chinese were 0.6 per cent and the Japanese 1.3 per cent.

In 1920 the total population in the city had increased to 576,673; the ratio of the Chinese population had dropped to 0.4 per cent and that of the Japanese had risen to 2.0 per cent.

The proportion of the Oriental arrests of the total population in the city each year is as follows:

TABLE 29

PERCENTAGE OF CHINESE AND JAPANESE ARRESTED TO TOTAL POPULATION IN
LOS ANGELES (CITY), 1914–1927

Year	Number of Orientals Arrested		Total Population	Percentage of Total Population		
	Chinese	Japanese		Chinese	Japanese	Total
1914.........	477	624	319,198 (1910)	0.15	0.20	0.35
1915.........	306	431		0.10	0.13	0.23
1916.........	721	771		0.23	0.24	0.47
1917.........	485	781		0.15	0.24	0.39
1918.........	570	1,033		0.18	0.32	0.50
1919.........	838	1,295		0.26	0.40	0.66
1920.........	516	997	576,673 (1920)	0.09	0.17	0.26
1921.........	491	312		0.09	0.05	0.14
1922.........	412	377		0.07	0.07	0.14
1923.........	584	412		0.10	0.07	0.17
1924.........	816	576		0.14	0.10	0.24
1925.........	1,040	754		0.18	0.13	0.31
1926.........	588	620		0.10	0.11	0.21
1927.........	1,146	1,133		0.20	0.20	0.40
Total.......	8,990	10,116	....	0.15	0.17	0.32

The average proportion of Chinese arrested to the total population in the city, since 1914, is 0.15 per cent, a fraction over one-tenth of 1 per cent; and the Japanese average is 0.17 per cent. The highest point for the Chinese arrested population in the city is 0.26 per cent in 1919, and the highest point for the Japanese is 0.4 per cent in 1919. In no other year did the combined number of Chinese and Japanese arrests reach even as high as one-half of 1 per cent; the average for the entire fourteen-year period of the proportion of Oriental arrests to total city population is 0.32 per cent.

Oakland.—In 1910 the population of Oakland totaled 150,174. Of this total the Oriental population was 3.4 per cent, that of the Chinese being 2.4 and of the Japanese 1.0 per cent.

In 1920 the total population in the city was 216,261. The Oriental population was then: Chinese, 1.8 per cent, and Japanese, 1.3 per cent; together, 3.1 per cent of the total.

During the 1910 census period the average of the Oriental arrested population constituted 0.16 per cent, made up of Chinese, 0.12 per cent, and Japanese, 0.04 per cent. During the 1920 census period the Chinese average percentage of arrested to total general population was 0.10, and the Japanese, 0.06. And during the entire fourteen-year period, the percentage of Chinese arrests to total population did not exceed 0.18 and of Japanese 0.10.

TABLE 30

PERCENTAGE OF CHINESE AND JAPANESE ARRESTED TO TOTAL POPULATION IN OAKLAND, 1914–1927

Year	Number of Orientals Arrested		Total Population	Percentage of Total Population		
	Chinese	Japanese		Chinese	Japanese	Total
1914..........	185	69	150,174 (1910)	0.12	0.05	0.17
1915..........	274	63		0.18	0.04	0.22
1916..........	121	78		0.08	0.05	0.13
1917..........	145	58		0.10	0.04	0.14
1918..........	123	57		0.08	0.04	0.12
1919..........	258	54		0.17	0.04	0.21
1920..........	390	128	216,261 (1920)	0.18	0.06	0.24
1921..........	270	156		0.12	0.07	0.19
1922..........	226	214		0.10	0.10	0.20
1923..........	192	166		0.09	0.08	0.17
1924..........	145	124		0.07	0.06	0.13
1925..........	125	64		0.06	0.03	0.09
1926..........	141	50		0.07	0.02	0.09
1927..........	211	81		0.10	0.04	0.14
Total.......	2,806	1,362	....	0.11	0.05	0.16

San Jose.—The general population of San Jose increased from 28,946 in 1910 to 39,642 in 1920. The proportion of the Oriental population during these two decades decreased: from 1.2 per cent to 0.9 per cent for the Chinese, and from 1.2 to 0.9 per cent for the Japanese. It is interesting to observe what proportion of the city population their volume of arrests constitute each year.

TABLE 31

PERCENTAGE OF CHINESE AND JAPANESE ARRESTED TO TOTAL POPULATION IN SAN JOSE, 1914–1927

Year	Number of Orientals Arrested		Total Population	Percentage of Total Population		
	Chinese	Japanese		Chinese	Japanese	Total
1914.........	50	13	28,946 (1910)	0.17	0.04	0.21
1915.........	57	22		0.20	0.08	0.28
1916.........	75	26		0.26	0.09	0.35
1917.........	92	34		0.32	0.12	0.44
1918.........	60	51		0.21	0.18	0.39
1919.........	40	16		0.14	0.06	0.20
1920.........	38	28	39,642 (1920)	0.10	0.07	0.17
1921.........	60	23		0.15	0.06	0.21
1922.........	59	37		0.15	0.09	0.24
1923.........	539	77		1.36	0.19	1.55
1924.........	61	58		0.15	0.14	0.29
1925.........	50	50		0.13	0.13	0.26
1926.........	95	122		0.24	0.30	0.54
1927.........	96	155		0.24	0.39	0.63
Total.......	1,372	711	....	0.24	0.14	0.38

The average for the period from 1914–1927 is for the Chinese 0.24 per cent, and for the Japanese 0.14 per cent. In 1923, when there seems to have been a large number of raids in the Oriental quarters, the proportion of the Chinese arrested population to the total general population in the city was 1.4 per cent, equaling the general ratio of their population in the city. Otherwise, in each year, the number of Orientals arrested formed but a fraction of 1 per cent of the population.

Sacramento (*city*).—The total population in Sacramento in 1920 was 65,908, and the Orientals in it constitute altogether 4.3 per cent, the Chinese being 1.3 and the Japanese 3.0 per cent.

The arrest records for the city of Sacramento cover the period since 1921, therefore the 1920 census figures are used.

During the seven-year period 1921–1927 the Orientals arrested formed an average of 0.31, a little over three-tenths of 1 per cent of the total population in the city: the Chinese 0.21 per cent, and the Japanese 0.10 per cent.

TABLE 32

PERCENTAGE OF CHINESE AND JAPANESE ARRESTED TO TOTAL POPULATION IN
SACRAMENTO (CITY), 1921–1927

Year	Number of Orientals Arrested		Total Population	Percentage of Total Population		
	Chinese	Japanese		Chinese	Japanese	Total
1921..........	184	129	65,908 (1920)	0.28	0.20	0.48
1922..........	113	73		0.17	0.11	0.28
1923..........	182	45		0.28	0.07	0.35
1924..........	133	42		0.20	0.06	0.26
1925..........	174	47		0.26	0.07	0.33
1926..........	85	54		0.13	0.08	0.21
1927..........	100	83		0.15	0.13	0.28
Total.......	971	473	....	0.21	0.10	0.31

Stockton.—In Stockton the Chinese constitute 2.7 per cent and the Japanese 2.1 per cent of the total population in the city, which numbered 40,296 in 1920.

Of the total population of Stockton during the period 1925 to 1927, the Oriental population arrested by the police for various offenses were 0.92, or a fraction over nine-tenths of 1 per cent. The Chinese arrested were 0.82 and the Japanese 0.10 per cent of the total population in the city.

TABLE 33

NUMBER AND PERCENTAGE OF CHINESE AND JAPANESE ARRESTED IN
STOCKTON, 1925–1927

Year	Number of Orientals Arrested		Total Population	Percentage of Total Population		
	Chinese	Japanese		Chinese	Japanese	Total
1925..........	200	44	40,296 (1920)	0.50	0.11	0.61
1926..........	581	64		1.40	0.16	1.56
1927..........	225	15		0.56	0.04	0.60
Total.......	1,006	123	....	0.82	0.10	0.92

Sacramento County.—Sacramento County has a total population, according to the census report for 1920, of 91,029; and the Oriental population constitutes 8.5 per cent—the Chinese 2.1 per cent, and the Japanese 6.4 per cent.

In 1910 the population of the county was 67,806 and at that time the Chinese formed 3.1 per cent and the Japanese 5.7 per cent of the total.

With the general Oriental population constituting at both periods over

8 per cent of the total county population, the following figures on the numbers and percentages arrested offer an interesting comparison.

TABLE 34

PERCENTAGE OF CHINESE AND JAPANESE ARRESTED TO TOTAL POPULATION IN
SACRAMENTO COUNTY, 1917–1927

Year	Number of Orientals Arrested		Total Population	Percentage of Total Population		
	Chinese	Japanese		Chinese	Japanese	Total
1917..........	63	10	67,806 (1910)	0.09	0.01	0.10
1918..........	18	11		0.03	0.02	0.05
1919..........	86	17		0.13	0.03	0.16
1920..........	90	6	91,029 (1920)	0.10	0.01	0.11
1921..........	58	18		0.06	0.02	0.08
1922..........	111	13		0.12	0.01	0.13
1923..........	125	11		0.14	0.01	0.15
1924..........	138	15		0.15	0.01	0.16
1925..........	43	33		0.05	0.03	0.08
1926..........	41	6		0.04	0.01	0.05
1927..........	59	28		0.06	0.03	0.09
Total.......	832	168	....	0.09	0.02	0.11

For both races the average is about one-tenth of 1 per cent for the entire period, 1917 to 1927, 11 years. The Japanese arrests are so few in number that the percentage calculation is almost negligible, and the average for both was brought up to the fraction of 1 per cent by the larger number of Chinese arrests each year. And for each race the ratio of their arrested numbers to the total population comes to fractions of one-tenth and one-fiftieth of 1 per cent each year.

Fresno County.—Fresno County, like Sacramento County, is an important Oriental settlement, chiefly Japanese. In 1910, of its 75,657 of general population, the Chinese were 1.8 and the Japanese 3.0 per cent. In 1920, of its 128,779 total population, the Chinese formed 0.8 and the Japanese 4.5 per cent.

On page 44 is seen what part of the population the Oriental arrests were every year since 1914.

In Fresno County, for the period 1914 to 1927, the average of arrests to total population is for the Chinese 0.10, and for the Japanese 0.05 per cent. The highest point for the Chinese is 0.26 per cent in 1925, and for the Japanese 0.13 per cent in 1917. Otherwise the ratio each year for the Chinese runs from one-tenth to two-tenths of 1 per cent and for the Japanese, closely calculated as possible, the ratios approximate a twentieth of 1 per cent of the total population in the county.

TABLE 35

PERCENTAGE OF CHINESE AND JAPANESE ARRESTED TO TOTAL POPULATION IN
FRESNO COUNTY, 1914–1927

Year	Number of Orientals Arrested		Total Population	Percentage of Total Population		
	Chinese	Japanese		Chinese	Japanese	Total
1914.........	44	15	75,657 (1910)	0.06	0.02	0.08
1915.........	112	30		0.15	0.04	0.19
1916.........	140	55		0.19	0.07	0.26
1917.........	177	100		0.23	0.13	0.36
1918.........	59	29		0.08	0.04	0.12
1919.........	88	30		0.12	0.04	0.16
1920.........	47	31	128,779 (1920)	0.04	0.02	0.06
1921.........	76	28		0.06	0.02	0.08
1922.........	90	48		0.07	0.04	0.11
1923.........	36	57		0.03	0.04	0.07
1924.........	131	66		0.10	0.05	0.15
1925.........	331	73		0.26	0.06	0.32
1926.........	86	72		0.07	0.06	0.13
1927.........	55	26		0.04	0.02	0.06
Total.......	1,472	660	....	0.10	0.05	0.15

Santa Clara County.—In Santa Clara County the Orientals form, according to the 1920 census rating, 3.8 per cent of the total population: the

TABLE 36

PERCENTAGE OF CHINESE AND JAPANESE ARRESTED TO TOTAL POPULATION IN
SANTA CLARA COUNTY, 1917–1927

Year	Number of Orientals Arrested		Total Population	Percentage of Total Population		
	Chinese	Japanese		Chinese	Japanese	Total
1917.........	2	1	83,539 (1910)	0.00	0.00	0.00
1918.........	16	1		0.02	0.00	0.02
1919.........	79	3		0.09	0.00	0.09
1920.........	15	6	100,676 (1920)	0.01	0.01	0.02
1921.........	24	7		0.02	0.01	0.03
1922.........	15	9		0.01	0.01	0.02
1923.........	13	5		0.01	0.00	0.01
1924.........	35	4		0.03	0.00	0.03
1925.........	39	8		0.04	0.01	0.05
1926.........	31	4		0.03	0.00	0.03
1927.........	125	3		0.12	0.00	0.12
Total	394	51	....	0.04	0.005	0.045

Chinese 0.8, and the Japanese 3.0 per cent. The total number of the general population in the county was 100,676.

In 1910 the total general population was 83,539, and the Chinese formed 1.3, the Japanese 2.7 per cent.

The proportion of Japanese arrests to total general population is so small as to render accurate calculation impossible. The average of the Chinese arrests for the period 1917–1927 is 0.04 per cent. The highest point is in 1927, when it was a little over one-tenth of 1 per cent.

San Joaquin County.—In San Joaquin County a large and industrious settlement of Japanese is situated. The total population in the county is 79,905. The Japanese constitute 5.4 per cent of the total population, and, although much decreased in numbers from earlier times, the Chinese still form 2.3 per cent of the total population in the county.

It was possible to procure data covering only the three years 1924 to 1926 inclusive, and the following calculation is based on the 1920 census.

TABLE 37

PERCENTAGE OF CHINESE AND JAPANESE ARRESTED TO TOTAL POPULATION IN
SAN JOAQUIN COUNTY, 1924–1926

Year	Number of Orientals Arrested		Total Population	Percentage of Total Population		
	Chinese	Japanese		Chinese	Japanese	Total
1924.........	138	4	79,905 (1920)	0.17	0.01	0.18
1925.........	109	11		0.14	0.01	0.15
1926.........	229	14		0.29	0.02	0.31
Total.......	476	29	....	0.20	0.01	0.21

Of the entire population Oriental arrests form 0.21 per cent, and of these the Chinese represent 0.20 per cent. The number of Japanese arrests, when related to the volume of population in the county, is insignificant.

Imperial County.—Imperial County did not appear in the census report until 1910. At that time the volume of population in the whole county was 13,591, the Chinese forming 0.2 per cent and the Japanese 1.5 per cent. In 1920 the total of population had increased to 43,453, the ratio of Chinese population remaining the same, 0.2 per cent, but the Japanese ratio had increased to 4.6 per cent.

The following data on Orientals arrested, starting with the year 1914, are therefore based on the *Census Reports* of 1910 and 1920 of population.

The average proportion of arrests to total population for the period 1914–1927 is the same for both races: 0.06 per cent. In 1919 the Japanese had the highest point, 0.26, and in 1921 the Chinese had 0.23 per cent, while, excepting 1927, when the Japanese had 0.15 per cent, neither reaches as high as one-tenth of 1 per cent in its proportion of arrested to total population.

TABLE 38

PERCENTAGE OF CHINESE AND JAPANESE ARRESTED TO TOTAL POPULATION IN IMPERIAL COUNTY, 1914–1927

Year	Number of Orientals Arrested		Total Population	Percentage of Total Population		
	Chinese	Japanese		Chinese	Japanese	Total
1914.........	11	1	13,591 (1910)	0.08	0.01	0.09
1915.........	19	4		0.14	0.03	0.17
1916.........	2	1		0.01	0.01	0.02
1917.........	5	2		0.04	0.01	0.05
1918.........	1	8		0.01	0.06	0.07
1919.........	9	36		0.07	0.26	0.33
1920.........	23	15	43,453 (1920)	0.05	0.03	0.08
1921.........	106	16		0.23	0.04	0.27
1922.........	7	15		0.02	0.03	0.05
1923.........	3	33		0.01	0.08	0.09
1924.........	11	29		0.03	0.07	0.10
1925.........	7	25		0.02	0.06	0.08
1926.........	30	21		0.07	0.05	0.12
1927.........	41	66		0.09	0.15	0.24
Total.......	275	272	....	0.06	0.06	0.12

Kern County.—In 1910, in Kern County, of 37,715 general population the Chinese constituted 2.2 per cent and the Japanese 0.7 per cent. In 1920 the population was 54,843, and the Chinese ratio had fallen to 1.0, the Japanese remaining at 0.6 per cent.

In this county also the number of Oriental arrests each year was so small that calculation of their ratio to total population is difficult; but some idea of the condition is portrayed in the following table.

It may be observed that the total Oriental population, though always quite small, reached its highest percentage of the total population of the county in 1914 (2.9 per cent), and in that year the total Oriental arrests were also higher than in any following year, being 86 in number. These were nearly all (79) Chinese, since the total Japanese population in the county has always been insignificant.

TABLE 39

PERCENTAGE OF CHINESE AND JAPANESE ARRESTED TO TOTAL POPULATION IN
KERN COUNTY, 1914–1927

Year	Number of Orientals Arrested		Total Population	Percentage of Total Population		
	Chinese	Japanese		Chinese	Japanese	Total
1914.........	77	9	37,715 (1910)	0.20	0.02	0.22
1915.........	39	..		0.10	....	0.10
1916.........	31	2		0.08	0.01	0.09
1917.........	22	..		0.06	....	0.06
1918.........	31	..		0.08	....	0.08
1919.........	7	..		0.02	....	0.02
1920.........	26	..	54,843 (1920)	0.04	....	0.04
1921.........	11	2		0.02	....	0.02
1922.........	9	..		0.02	....	0.02
1923.........	7	3		0.01	0.01	0.02
1924.........	7	..		0.01	....	0.01
1925.........	17	1		0.03	....	0.03
1926.........	20	..		0.04	....	0.04
1927.........	15	3		0.03	0.01	0.04
Total.......	319	20	....	0.05	0.00	0.05

Berkeley.—In the city of Berkeley the total population, according to the census of 1920, was estimated to be 56,036. The proportion of Chinese is 0.6 per cent and that of Japanese 1.6 per cent. In 1910 the population in the city was 40,434, and the Oriental ratio of the two races was as follows: 1.1 per cent for the Chinese and 1.8 per cent for the Japanese.

The number of arrests of Orientals in this city is, as in the other centers, relatively small; nevertheless an attempt is made to show in the following table the proportion their arrests have formed of the total population year by year, and the average for the entire period.

The average ratio of Oriental arrests to total population for the entire period 1914–1927 is 0.037. The Japanese arrests are more numerous than those of the Chinese, and the ratio to the total population is slightly higher in consequence, but for both the figures are such as cannot be seriously considered in meaning.

The Japanese arrests in Berkeley were 227 for the period covered, as compared to 91 Chinese arrests; much the largest numbers for single years were found in 1926 and 1927, 20 Chinese being arrested in 1926 and 58 Japanese in 1927. The combined number of Oriental arrests equaled 2.7 per cent of the total Oriental population, while total city arrests equaled 2.3 per cent of the total population.

TABLE 40

PERCENTAGE OF CHINESE AND JAPANESE ARRESTED TO TOTAL POPULATION IN
BERKELEY, 1914–1927

Year	Number of Orientals Arrested		Total Population	Percentage of Total Population		
	Chinese	Japanese		Chinese	Japanese	Total
1914.........	6	9	40,434 (1910)	0.015	0.022	0.037
1915.........	4	3		0.010	0.007	0.017
1916.........	4	3		0.010	0.007	0.017
1917.........	3	3		0.007	0.007	0.014
1918.........	4	19		0.010	0.047	0.057
1919.........	4	6		0.010	0.015	0.025
1920.........	1	7	56,036 (1920)	0.002	0.012	0.014
1921.........	9	10		0.016	0.018	0.034
1922.........	2	15		0.004	0.027	0.031
1923.........	..	10		.....	0.018	0.018
1924.........	9	9		0.016	0.016	0.032
1925.........	17	24		0.030	0.043	0.073
1926.........	20	51		0.036	0.091	0.127
1927.........	8	58		0.014	0.103	0.117
Total.......	91	227	....	0.013	0.024	0.037

SUMMARY: PERCENTAGE OF ORIENTAL ARRESTS TO TOTAL POPULATION

The volume of Oriental law-breakers lodged amid the total population of California cannot be considered as very significant. Examining the arrest data assembled from twenty-six centers in which the majority of the Oriental population is contained, it becomes evident that the percentage their arrests form of the total population in each center is relatively small. The table opposite brings this before us in summary detail.

From the foregoing it is seen that the highest ratio of Oriental arrests to total population occurs in the city of San Francisco, where the proportion is 1.2 per cent of the city population. At the same time it must be observed that the total Oriental population ratio to general population is 2.6 per cent, and though the frequency of arrests of Orientals in that city is high, the ratio of arrested population is nevertheless less than half of the general population ratio.

In all the centers the total arrests of Orientals are an almost insignificant figure and involve a very small portion of the general Oriental population ratio in each locality.

The place of the Oriental law-breaker in the communities of California is seen more clearly from another angle—when the ratio of Oriental ar-

TABLE 41

COMPARISON OF PERCENTAGES OF ORIENTAL POPULATION TO TOTAL POPULATION,
AND ORIENTAL ARRESTS TO TOTAL POPULATION IN 24 CENTERS
AT VARIOUS DATES

Period	Place	Percentage of Oriental Population			Percentage of Oriental Arrests		
		Chinese	Japanese	Total	Chinese	Japanese	Total
1918–28	San Francisco	1.5	1.1	2.6	0.9	0.3	1.2
1914–27	Los Angeles	0.4	2.0	2.4	0.15	0.17	0.32
1914–27	Oakland	1.8	1.3	3.1	0.11	0.05	0.16
1914–27	San Jose	0.9	0.8	1.7	0.24	0.14	0.38
1921–27	Sacramento (city)	1.3	3.0	4.3	0.21	0.10	0.31
1925–27	Stockton	2.7	2.1	4.8	0.82	0.10	0.92
1914–27	Berkeley	0.6	1.6	2.2	0.013	0.024	0.04
1917–27	Sacramento County	2.1	6.4	8.5	0.09	0.02	0.11
1914–27	Fresno County	0.8	4.5	5.3	0.10	0.05	0.15
1917–27	Santa Clara County	0.8	3.0	3.8	0.04	0.00	0.04
1924–26	San Joaquin County	2.3	5.4	7.7	0.20	0.01	0.21
1914–27	Imperial County	0.2	4.6	4.8	0.06	0.06	0.12
1914–27	Alameda County	1.3	1.5	2.8	....	....	....
1914–27	Kern County	1.0	0.6	1.6	0.05	....	0.05
1918–27	Santa Barbara County	0.8	2.3	3.1	....	....	....
1900–27	San Benito County	1.2	4.7	5.9	0.01	0.07	0.08
1900–27	Alameda (city)	0.3	2.2	2.5	....	....	0.30
1900–27	Orange County	...	2.4	2.4	....	....	0.01
1900–27	San Diego County	0.3	1.3	1.6	....	....	0.05
1900–27	Kings County	2.0	2.7	4.7	....	....	0.05
1914–27	Monterey County	2.7	5.8	8.5	....	0.03	0.03
1914–27	San Mateo County	0.9	1.8	2.7	0.01	0.01	0.02
1900–27	Sutter County	0.4	3.7	4.1	....	....	0.02
1900–27	San Quentin Prison	0.8	2.1	2.9	0.01	0.004	0.104

rests to total population is compared with the ratio of total arrests to total population in each center and for the state, as shown in Table 42 (p. 50).

From this comparison it is perceived that in each center the Orientals arrested prove to be but a fraction of the population when compared with the proportion contributed by other parts of the population. In each of the centers the total arrests ranged between 0.9 and 23.4 per cent; while the Orientals arrested therein formed but fractions of one per cent except in one city, namely, San Francisco, where the Oriental ratio was 1.2 per cent, while the total arrest ratio in this city was 9.1 per cent. The high rate of Oriental arrests in San Francisco is evidently to be related to the special character of "Chinatown" in this city until recent years, as is indicated by a comparison with the rate for Los Angeles, it being only 0.32 per cent of the population.

TABLE 42

COMPARISON OF RATIOS OF TOTAL ARRESTS AND ORIENTAL
ARRESTS TO TOTAL POPULATION IN 22 CENTERS

Period	Area	Percentage of All Arrests to Total Population	Percentage of Oriental Arrests to Total Population
1918–28	San Francisco....................	9.1	1.2
1914–27	Los Angeles.....................	12.1	0.32
1914–27	Oakland	10.1	0.16
1914–27	San Jose........................	10.0	0.38
1921–27	Sacramento (city)................	12.8	0.31
1925–27	Stockton (city)..................	23.4	0.92
1914–27	Berkeley	2.3	0.04
1914–27	Alameda County.................	3.0	0.06
1917–27	Sacramento County...............	14.7	0.11
1914–27	Fresno County...................	4.6	0.15
1914–27	Imperial County	4.7	0.12
1914–27	Kern County.....................	3.6	0.05
1925–27	San Joaquin County..............	8.1	0.22
1900–27	Alameda (city)..................	2.4	0.3
1900–27	San Diego County................	0.9	0.05
1914–27	San Mateo County................	2.5	0.02
1917–27	Santa Clara County..............	3.6*	0.04
1914–27	Monterey County.................	5.0*	0.03
1900–27	San Benito County...............	0.9	0.08
1900–27	Sutter County...................	0.7	0.02
1900–27	Kings County....................	0.9*	0.05
1900–27	Orange County...................	0.9*	0.01

* Estimated.

PERCENTAGE OF ORIENTAL ARRESTS TO ORIENTAL POPULATION

What proportion do the Oriental arrests constitute of the Oriental population in each center? In other words, what percentage of their own volume of population in each locality here examined were arrested each year; what is the average for the whole period considered, in each center and for the state? The table on the opposite page summarizes this condition.

For all serious, all anti-social offenses, San Quentin Prison must be taken as the indicator. To that institution the Orientals contributed 0.17 per cent of their volume of population in the state: of the Chinese total population, the proportion was 0.11 per cent, and the Japanese, 0.06 per cent, over a period of 27 years.

The proportion from among the Orientals studied who were committed to Folsom Prison during 1900–1927 was 0.13 per cent.

In the city of San Francisco the frequency of Oriental arrests is the highest; during the period 1918–1928, the number of arrests equaled 57.1 per cent of the total Oriental population in the city: 54.1 per cent from among the Chinese and 3.0 per cent from among the Japanese.

TABLE 43

PERCENTAGE OF ORIENTAL ARRESTS TO ORIENTAL TOTAL
POPULATION, BY PERIODS AND LOCALITIES

Period	Area	Percentage of Oriental Arrests to Total Oriental Population		
		Chinese	Japanese	Total
1900–27	San Quentin Prison	0.11	0.062	0.17
1900–27	Folsom Prison	...	...	0.13
1918–28	San Francisco (city)	54.1	3.0	57.1
1914–27	Los Angeles (city)	31.4	11.4	42.8
1914–27	Oakland	5.4	4.4	9.8
1914–27	San Jose	25.7	13.6	39.3
1914–27	Sacramento (city)	16.7	3.5	20.2
1925–27	Stockton	31.3	4.5	35.8
1914–27	Berkeley	0.8	1.9	2.7
1914–27	Alameda County	0.24	0.09	0.33
1914–27	Kern County	3.2	0.5	3.7
1917–27	Sacramento County	3.8	0.3	4.1
1914–27	Fresno County	9.3	1.3	10.6
1914–27	Imperial County	29.0	2.5	31.5
1917–27	Santa Clara County	4.4	0.18	4.6
1914–26	San Joaquin County	8.6	0.22	8.8
1914–27	Alameda (city)	...	...	5.2
1900–27	Orange County	...	...	0.4
1900–27	San Diego County	...	...	32.3
1900–27	Kings County	...	...	23.0
1900–27	Sutter County	...	...	0.2
1917–27	Santa Barbara (city)	...	...	11.3
1914–27	Monterey County	...	...	0.4
1900–27	San Benito County	...	...	0.2

In the city of Los Angeles, the number of arrests equaled 31.4 per cent of the Chinese, and 11.4 per cent of the Japanese population during 1914–1927. The figures for the other centers are readily ascertained from Table 43.

SUMMARY

According to the 1920 census of population, California possessed about three and one-half millions of people. Among these there were 28,812 Chinese, and 71,952 Japanese. Of the total population, the Chinese constituted eight-tenths of one per cent, and the Japanese a fraction over two per cent.

It was possible in this investigation to assemble official data on the volume of arrests made in twenty-six centers, comprising seventeen counties and nine cities. These centers represent 80 per cent of the total general population of the state and 89 per cent of the total Oriental population in the state. And among these centers are included all the important Oriental settlements in cities and counties.

The police reports show that in these localities, at various stated periods between 1900 and 1928, there were made over two million arrests, among which were 71,626 Chinese and 17,727 Japanese. Among these are included all commitments to San Quentin Prison made during the period 1900–1927. Of the two million general arrests made at intervals since 1900, the accumulated Oriental arrests constitute 4.4 per cent: the Chinese, 3.5, and the Japanese, 0.9. To arrive at a more accurate indication, it is necessary to examine each locality separately. Doing so, it is found that the highest percentage of Oriental arrests, as compared with the other centers, occurs in the city of San Francisco, where the proportion of the Chinese arrested to the total arrests is 10.1 per cent, and that of the Japanese, 0.3 per cent.

Of the total number of prisoners committed to San Quentin for serious offenses and long-term sentences between 1900 and 1927, the Chinese numbered 978 and the Japanese 364, constituting 1.76 and 0.65 per cent of the total convictions respectively.

Of the other centers of Oriental population,

a) Nine reported arrests made between 1900 and 1927 of which in each center the Oriental quota constituted a range between 0.2 and 6.5 per cent of the total arrests.

b) Ten reported arrests made between 1914 and 1927, of which in each center the Oriental quota formed between 0.6 per cent (the lowest) and 4.0 per cent (the highest) of the total arrests made.

c) Three reported arrests made between 1917 and 1927, of which the Orientals formed between 1.1 and 7.1 per cent of the total.

d) Three reported arrests made between 1921 and 1927, of which the Oriental quota constituted between 2.5 and 4.1 per cent of the total.

In four centers, the Oriental arrests constituted less than 1 per cent; in six centers from 1 to 2 per cent; in four centers from 3 to 4 per cent; in three centers from 4 to 5 per cent; in one center from 5 to 6 per cent; in one center 6.5 per cent; in one 7.1 per cent; and in one 10.4 per cent of the total arrests in that locality.

The range of the Chinese ratio to total arrests is: in seven centers they were less than 1 per cent of the total; in six centers they formed from 1 to 2 per cent of the total; in six centers they formed from 2 to 3 per cent of the total; in three centers they formed from 3 to 4 per cent of the total; in one center they formed from 4 to 5 per cent of the total; in one center they formed 5.9 per cent; and in one center they formed 10.1 per cent of the total arrests, which is their highest point.

The range of the Japanese ratio of arrests to total arrests in each center is as follows: in fifteen centers they constituted less than 1 per cent of the total; in eight centers they formed from 1 to 2 per cent of the total; and in two centers they formed from 2 to 3 per cent of the total, 3.0 per cent being their highest point.

From a review of the ratio of Chinese and Japanese arrests to total arrests in each locality for separate successive years, it is evident that the number of Orientals arrested in each year throughout the state is declining; from which it is safe to conclude that instead of being a source of increasing alarm to the authorities, and to the community in which they live, their conduct should tend rather to decrease this alarm. Neither, during the period under examination, did they constitute what can be called a dangerous proportion of the arrests and prison convictions in the state to date, nor is there any indication that this proportion is on the increase; on the contrary, the evidence shows that it is rather on the decrease.

Of the total population in the state, Oriental criminals form a proportion so small as to be difficult of accurate calculation year by year. For the entire period 1900–1927, the Orientals sent to San Quentin Prison constitute about one-hundredth of one per cent of the total population of the state. The figures for San Quentin must be taken as the only conclusive measurement of their serious criminal activities as such.

In the other centers, the Orientals arrested form but small fractions of one per cent of the total population in each, with but two exceptions: Thus, in San Francisco the Orientals arrested equal 1.2 per cent, and in the city of Stockton they equal 0.92 per cent, of the total population. In contrast, the total arrests made in each locality range up to 23 per cent.

The question, what proportion the Oriental arrests form of their own population in each center, shows up the frequency of arrests, and here it is seen that the highest frequency occurs in the large cities and, for the reason later indicated, the border counties: thus, in San Francisco the Oriental arrests equal 57.1 per cent of the total Oriental population; in Los Angeles 42.8 per cent; in San Jose 39.3 per cent; in the city of Stockton 35.8 per cent; in the city of Sacramento 20.2 per cent; in Imperial County 31.5 per cent; and in San Diego County 32.3 per cent. In the other localities the range is from 0.2 per cent to 11 per cent.

Explanation for such frequencies, especially as is seen from the detailed tables above, among the Oriental population, is given in the succeeding chapter, in which is analyzed the nature of the offenses for which arrests were made.

IV. ANALYSIS OF ORIENTAL OFFENSES

Classification of offenses.—The Penal Code[1] divides offenses into four classes:

I. Offenses against the person
II. Offenses against public policy and morals
III. Offenses against public health and safety
IV. Offenses against property

In the first class are offenses of personal violence, such as murder, rape, assault and battery, robbery, libel, extortion, etc. In the second class are all those offenses which are meant to do harm to the person and which break statutes and local ordinances, such as bribery, gaming, smuggling, etc. In the third class are included such acts as would be injurious to public health and safety, such as fire, health, and traffic violations, rioting, disturbing the peace, carrying firearms, etc. And in the fourth class are acts harmful to the safety of property, such as larceny, burglary, fraud, forgery, etc.

This is accepted as the ordinary classification of crime, by which may be measured the effect of the criminal act upon society.

The Federal Commission on Immigration in 1910, when investigating the question of immigration and crime, made another classification, for the reason that ". . . . the customary classification of crimes into offenses against the person, property, etc., while sufficiently indicating the immediate effect of the criminal act upon society, does not sufficiently describe the character of the offender. A modification therefore was made of the classification for the purpose of indicating more clearly the character of the offenders themselves."

The Commission's grouping of offenses is:

1. Gainful offenses—Blackmail and extortion, burglary, forgery, larceny, receiving stolen goods, and robbery
2. Offenses of violence—Abduction and kidnapping, assault, homicide, and rape
3. Offenses against public policy—Disorderly conduct, gaming, vagrancy, etc.
4. Offenses against chastity—Prostitution, etc.
5. Unclassified offenses—Abandonment, abortion, arson, attempted suicide, cruelty, malicious behavior, etc.

---

[1] *Senate Document No. 750, 61st Congress, Third Session, 1910–11,* Vol. 18, "Immigration and Crime," p. 10.

It was thought that it might be worth while in this study to classify the data on Oriental offenses according to each of the foregoing methods. According to the Penal Code classification, there is the possibility of measuring to what extent the Oriental offender is a menace to society. And according to the Immigration Commission's classification, there is the promise of "throwing some light on their characters." However, the results of the two classifications, as far as this study is concerned, were found to be essentially the same, and therefore the tables based on the Immigration Commission's classification are omitted, except that certain totals are given in the summary of this chapter for purposes of comparison.

Penal Code classification: Oriental offenses.—The following is an analysis of the types of offenses for which Orientals have been arrested in various centers throughout the state, based upon records of arrests by California police. The number of offenses here enumerated, each represented by an arrest, is somewhat smaller than the number of arrests indicated in the preceding chapter, for the reason that returns from some police offices indicate the number of arrests made but do not give accompanying explanatory data. The difference, however, is slight enough not to cause any change of consequence in the calculations involved.

TABLE 44

DISTRIBUTION OF CRIMES OF ORIENTALS ACCORDING TO
PENAL CODE CLASSIFICATION

Classification	Chinese		Japanese		Total	
	Number	Percent-age	Number	Percent-age	Number	Percent-age
I. Offenses against the person....	671	1.03	393	2.30	1,064	1.30
II. Offenses against public policy and morals..................	53,322	82.05	7,275	42.54	60,597	73.82
III. Offenses against public health and safety..................	10,366	15.95	8,803	51.47	19,169	23.35
IV. Offenses against property......	626	.96	632	3.70	1,258	1.53
Total	64,985	100.00	17,103	100.00	82,088	100.00

Out of a total of 64,985 offenses, the Chinese committed 671 offenses against the person, or 1.03 per cent of the total; 53,322 offenses against public policy and morals, constituting 82.05 per cent of the total; 10,366 offenses against public health and safety, or 15.95 per cent of the total; and 626 offenses against property, comprising 0.96 per cent of the total.

The Japanese offenses total 17,103. Of these, 393 were against the person, forming 2.30 per cent of the total; 7,275 were against public policy and morals, forming 42.54 per cent of the total; 8,803 were against public health and safety, or 51.47 per cent of the total; and 632 were against property, forming 3.70 per cent of the total.

Adding the number of offenses committed by both races under the heading "Oriental Offenses," we find that 1,064 out of a total of 82,088 were offenses against the person, forming 1.30 per cent of the total; 60,597 were against public policy and morals, forming 73.82 per cent of the total; 19,169 were against public health and safety, or 23.35 per cent of the total; and 1,258 were against property, forming 1.53 per cent of the total number of offenses.

The points to remark are: the small number of offenses against the person and against property, and the large number of offenses against public policy and morals and against public health and safety.

The following tables show in detail the contents of these classifications by which it is possible to understand their significance as regards the intent of the offenders.

TABLE 45

NUMBER AND PERCENTAGE OF CRIMES AGAINST THE PERSON

Classification	Chinese		Japanese	
	Number	Percent-age	Number	Percent-age
Homicide	231	0.36	95	0.56
Injury	42	0.06	38	0.22
Assault	188	0.29	106	0.62
Battery	117	0.18	133	0.78
Robbery	81	0.12	8	0.05
Kidnapping	...	....	1	0.01
Conspiracy to murder	3	....	...	....
Libel	4	0.01	2	0.01
Highway robbery	...	....	1	0.01
Hold-up	...	....	2	0.01
Pickpocket	1	....	...	....
Threats against life	4	0.01	7	0.04
Total	671	1.03	393	2.31

The ratio of each offense to total number of offenses in this classification is higher in most cases for the Japanese than for the Chinese. Out of a total of 671 offenses against the person, the Chinese committed 231 of homicide, constituting 0.36 per cent, and the Japanese committed 95 cases of homicide out of a total of 393 offenses, constituting 0.56 per cent. For battery, the Chinese ratio is 0.18 per cent, and the Japanese 0.78 per cent. For assault, the Chinese ratio is 0.29 per cent, and the Japanese 0.62 per cent. In robbery the Chinese percentage is higher, being 0.12 per cent, and that of the Japanese 0.05 per cent. For effecting injuries, the Chinese ratio is 0.06 and the Japanese 0.22 per cent. For libel, both have a low number and ratio, as also for threats against life. There is one case of a highway robbery for the Japanese, and two hold-up cases for them, while the Chinese have 3 cases of conspiracy to murder.

TABLE 46

OFFENSES OF ORIENTALS AGAINST THE PERSON, PUBLIC
POLICY, AND MORALS

Classification	Chinese		Japanese	
	Number	Percentage	Number	Percentage
Abandoning wife....................	1	....	..	....
Abortion	..	....	2	0.01
Bigamy	1	....	..	....
Adultery	2	....	10	0.06
Bribery	10	0.02	16	0.09
Crime against children.............	6	0.01	1	0.01
Cruelty to animals.................	43	0.07	44	0.26
Indecent exposure.................	9	0.01	5	0.03
Obscene literature and pictures......	2	....	9	0.05
Lewd and lascivious acts...........	11	0.02	1	0.01
Rape	9	0.01	4	0.02
Rape, suspect.....................	7	0.01	3	0.02
Digging up dead body..............	1	....	..	....
Gaming	14,855	22.86	2,699	15.78
Lottery	28,670	44.12	527	3.08
Smuggling	66	0.10	13	0.08
Vagrancy	3,359	5.17	263	1.54
Prostitution	230	0.35	52	0.30
Pimping..........................	2	....	..	....
Failure to provide.................	12	0.02	8	0.05
Interfering with officer.............	24	0.04	14	0.08
Violating immigration laws..........	1,605	2.47	149	0.87
Perjury	10	0.02	12	0.07
Violating liquor laws...............	486	0.75	1,041	6.09
Pandering	3	....	3	0.02
Soliciting	5	0.01	3	0.02
Suicide attempts...................	3	....	17	0.10
Seduction	1	....	..	....
Felony	89	0.14	39	0.23
Syndicalism	1	....	5	0.03
State wages law...................	11	0.02	5	0.03
Child labor law...................	7	0.01	4	0.02

TABLE 46 (*Continued*)

Classification	Chinese		Japanese	
	Number	Percent-age	Number	Percent-age
State labor law.....................	12	0.02	19	0.11
White slavery......................	2	....	2	0.01
Failure to render aid...............	..	....	2	0.01
Unlawful assembly..................	85	0.13	6	0.04
Mann Act..........................	..	....	1	0.01
Alien land law.....................	..	....	6	0.04
Deserter	18	0.03	..	....
Slacker	5	0.01	4	0.02
Selective service act................	41	0.06	..	....
Vulgar language....................	..	....	2	0.01
Contributing to delinquency.........	50	0.08	13	0.08
Juvenile delinquency...............	8	0.01	8	0.05
Juvenile court law..................	3	....	..	....
Malicious mischief..................	9	0.01	20	0.12
Malicious behavior..................	2	....	..	....
State medical laws..................	163	0.25	61	0.36
Parole violation	6	0.01	1	0.01
Probation law violation..............	23	0.04	12	0.07
Contempt of court..................	3	....	1	0.01
Assisting to escape.................	1	....	..	....
Hit-and-run	1	....	..	....
Incorrigibility	3	....	..	....
Selling tobacco to minor............	..	....	3	0.02
License ordinances..................	64	0.10	130	0.76
Registration ordinance..............	3	....	105	0.61
United States Revenue Act..........	1	....	..	....
United States Customs Act..........	6	0.01	..	....
Miscellaneous state misdemeanors....	185	0.28	105	0.61
Miscellaneous city ordinances........	3,087	4.75	1,825	10.67
Total	53,322	82.05	7,275	42.57

In this classification, the Chinese tend to exceed the Japanese in number and percentage, being responsible for 53,322 offenses against public policy as compared with but 7,275 for the Japanese. Their ratio to total offenses is almost double that of the Japanese: 82.05 per cent, to 42.57 per cent of the Japanese.

It is of interest to examine the details of this situation. There are seven distinct offenses for which each race shows a large number of arrests. These are: Gaming, for which the Chinese have 14,855 arrests and the Japanese 2,699; lottery playing, for which the Chinese have 28,670 arrests and the Japanese 527; vagrancy, for which the Chinese have 3,359 arrests and the Japanese 263; violation of immigration laws, for which the Chinese have 1,605 arrests and the Japanese 149; violation of liquor laws, for which the Chinese have 486 arrests and the Japanese 1,041; and violations of city ordinances, for which the Chinese have 3,087 arrests and the Japanese 1,825.

Gaming and lottery playing are for the Chinese the two major offenses, constituting the highest percentage classes, 22.86 and 44.12, respectively, totaling 66.98; these are followed by vagrancy, violation of immigration laws, and violation of city ordinances. All these form 79.37 per cent of the total offenses in this class.

Gaming, violation of liquor laws, and violation of city ordinances are for the Japanese the major offenses, constituting 31.93 per cent all together; these are followed by lottery playing and vagrancy. All these form 36.55 per cent of the 42.57 per cent total of this class of offenses.

The other offenses, of a miscellaneous character, such as perjury, bribery, smuggling, etc., do not, for either race, reach a full one per cent in each item. For the Chinese the remaining miscellany of offenses constitute about three per cent and those for the Japanese about six per cent of the total offenses in this category. Among these, the violation of state medical laws and miscellaneous state misdemeanors form the highest percentages. The Chinese have 163 arrests for violating state medical laws, constituting 0.25 per cent, and the Japanese have 61 such offenses, constituting 0.36 per cent. Of miscellaneous state misdemeanors, the Chinese have 185, forming 0.28 per cent, and the Japanese 105, forming 0.61 per cent of the total offenses in this class. For the Japanese next in order come 130 violations of license ordinances and 105 violations of registration ordinances.

Of specific moral offenses involving sex relations the numbers are small, ranging for the Chinese from 230 arrests for prostitution to 2 arrests for white slavery, and for the Japanese 52 arrests for prostitution to 1 arrest for lewd and lascivious acts.

In the Penal Code classification of offenses against public health and safety the percentage of Japanese offenses is higher than that of Chinese, being 51.47 for the former and 15.95 for the latter. But the total number of offenses against the public health and safety is 1,563 less for the Japanese than for the Chinese.

Taken separately, the major Chinese offense is violation of the opium and narcotic laws, which constitutes 11.75 out of the total of 15.95 per cent of this class, or is responsible for about three-fourths of the arrests for offenses against public health and safety.

The major offenses of the Japanese in this class are drunkenness and violations of traffic rules, which constitute together 37.38 out of the total 51.47 per cent, thus accounting for more than two-thirds of the total arrests in this category.

TABLE 47

OFFENSES OF ORIENTALS AGAINST PUBLIC HEALTH AND SAFETY

Classification	Chinese		Japanese	
	Number	Percent-age	Number	Percent-age
Opium and narcotics................	7,635	11.75	137	0.80
Disturbing the peace................	281	0.43	234	1.37
Drunkenness	213	0.33	1,853	10.83
Health ordinance violations..........	49	0.08	72	0.42
Fire ordinance violations............	10	0.02	39	0.23
Pure food act violations.............	73	0.11	42	0.25
Garbage ordinance violations........	4	0.01	122	0.71
Maintaining public nuisance........	7	0.01	4	0.02
State revolver act..................	138	0.21	3	0.02
Traffic ordinance violations..........	681	1.05	4,540	26.55
Carrying concealed weapons........	185	0.28	50	0.29
Carrying firearms..................	22	0.03	..	....
Insanity	154	0.24	132	0.77
Rioting	...	....	2	0.01
Unlawful assembly..................	85	0.13	6	0.04
Criminal negligence................	...	....	2	0.01
Criminal conspiracy................	...	....	2	0.01
No flu mask.......................	157	0.24	..	....
Medical treatment..................	169	0.26	572	3.34
Milk ordinance violations...........	1	....	32	0.19
Street and sidewalk ordinances......	298	0.46	413	2.41
Fruit and fruitstand ordinances......	...	....	62	0.36
Irrigation ordinance................	...	....	10	0.06
Fish and game laws................	38	0.06	222	1.30
Pilot ordinance....................	...	....	1	0.01
State apple law....................	...	....	36	0.21
Standardization act	3	....	24	0.14
Suspicious character	22	0.03	9	0.05
Investigation	71	0.11	47	0.27
Building ordinance violations........	11	0.02	..	....
Bicycle ordinance violations........	30	0.05	95	0.56
Barred-door ordinance..............	...	....	2	0.01
Curfew law........................	3	....	2	0.01
Condemned dance hall..............	1	....	1	0.01
Net container ordinance.............	...	....	4	0.02
Hotel and lodging ordinance........	2	....	10	0.06
Laundry ordinance..................	6	0.01	..	....
Poolroom ordinance................	...	....	10	0.06
Quarantine ordinance...............	17	0.03	5	0.03
Plumbing ordinance................	...	....	3	0.02
Harbor reserve ordinance...........	...	....	3	0.02
Total	10,366	15.95	8,803	51.47

The Japanese exceed the Chinese in offenses against the public peace, in violations of street and sidewalk ordinances, health and garbage ordinances, fish and game laws, fruit and fruitstand ordinances, and rules for medical treatment of ailments affecting public health and safety.

The Chinese rank higher than the Japanese in the commission of offenses against the flu-mask ordinance, the state revolver act, carrying concealed weapons and firearms, insanity or suspicions of insanity, and unlawful assembly.

Both races have a minor number of arrests for suspicion and investigation, and violations of bicycle ordinances, curfew law, hotel and lodgings ordinances, laundry, poolroom, quarantine, plumbing, and other such local ordinances.

TABLE 48

OFFENSES OF ORIENTALS AGAINST PROPERTY

Classification	Chinese		Japanese	
	Number	Percentage	Number	Percentage
Arson	2	....	6	0.04
Burglary	111	0.17	73	0.43
Forgery	27	0.04	51	0.30
Counterfeiting	1	....	1	0.01
Fraud	32	0.05	17	0.10
Conspiracy to defraud.............	1	....	..	....
Receiving stolen goods.............	13	0.02	4	0.02
Larceny (petty and grand)..........	254	0.39	174	1.02
Embezzlement	66	0.10	32	0.19
Extortion	6	0.01	4	0.02
Fictitious checks..................	38	0.06	84	0.49
Usury	..	....	1	0.01
Weights and measures ordinances....	75	0.12	185	1.08
Total	626	0.96	632	3.70

For offenses against property, the Japanese have a higher percentage rank than the Chinese and about equal them in number of arrests. In almost every item in this class the Japanese percentage is higher than that of the Chinese. Thus, for burglary and suspected burglary, the Japanese arrests constitute 0.43 per cent and the Chinese 0.17 per cent. For larceny, the Japanese figure is 1.02 per cent and the Chinese 0.39 per cent. For forgery, embezzlement, extortion, and counterfeiting, they are about equal; but for fictitious checks, weights and measures violations, and fraud the Japanese are higher than the Chinese.

But it should be noted that with the exception of violations against weights and measures ordinances and for larceny, where the Japanese percentage reaches the total of 1 per cent, neither race comes nearer than from one-half to 1 per cent of its total number of arrests for all offenses.

Detailed Penal Code Classification of Oriental Offenses

Does this brief record of offenses throw any light upon the nature of Oriental criminality in California? An attempt to answer this question is made in the summary below.

CHINESE OFFENSES

1. Acts that would directly menace human life and be destructive of personal safety total 671 out of a grand total of 64,985 Chinese offenses, constituting 1.03 per cent of the total.

2. Acts that would directly menace the safety of property and personal possessions total 626 out of a grand total of 64,985 Chinese offenses, constituting 0.96 per cent of the total.

3. Acts that would in a direct or an indirect way be injurious to public health and public safety total a little over ten thousand (10,366) out of a grand total of 64,985 Chinese offenses, constituting 15.95 per cent of the total. Among these, the most numerous are the violations of the opium and narcotics acts, and of traffic regulations, totaling over eight thousand, out of the ten thousand offenses in this class. In the remainder there are arrests for disturbing the peace, drunkenness, violations of liquor laws and pure food laws, the carrying of weapons, insanity, carelessness in the time of the influenza epidemic, violations of street and sidewalk ordinances and of ordinances for medical treatment for ailments affecting public safety. None of these, however, are of such volume as to become directly or immediately destructive of the public safety.

4. Acts that would be counter to the safety of the person in a less direct way than sheer violence, and be against public policy and morals as expressed by state acts or by city and county ordinances, are the most numerous among the Chinese offenses, totaling 53,322 out of the grand total of 64,985, and constituting 82.05 per cent of the total. The most numerous in this class are arrests for gambling and lottery playing, constituting almost forty-four thousand out of the total of approximately fifty-three thousand arrests in this classification. The next most numerous in rank are vagrancy, and violations of immigration laws, which together constitute an addition of almost five thousand arrests, totaling in all, for these four classes of offenses, forty-nine thousand out of the fifty-three thousand total. There remain about four thousand arrests distributed among a variety of some fifty-seven offenses listed in this classification.

JAPANESE OFFENSES

1. Acts that would directly destroy or menace human life and personal safety total 393 out of a grand total of 17,103 Japanese arrests, and constitute 2.30 per cent of the total.

2. Acts that would directly menace the safety of property and personal possessions total 632 out of a grand total of 17,103 Japanese arrests and constitute 3.70 per cent of the total.

3. Acts that would directly or indirectly be injurious to public health and safety total 8,803 out of a grand total of 17,103 Japanese arrests and constitute 51.47 per cent of the total. Among these, forty-five hundred, or about half of the total in this class, are sundry violations of traffic rules; over eighteen hundred are arrests for drunkenness; and almost six hundred concern registration for treatment of diseases affecting the public safety. Then there are over two hundred arrests for disturbing the peace, over one hundred for violations of garbage ordinances, over four hundred for street and sidewalk ordinances, over two hundred for fish and game laws, and a minor number for miscellaneous offenses of a like character.

4. Acts that would run counter to public policy and morals total a little over seven thousand (7,275) out of the grand total of 17,103 Japanese arrests, and constitute 42.5 per cent of the total. Among these, gaming totals almost twenty-seven hundred, lottery playing totals over five hundred, and violations of liquor laws total a little over one thousand, making up a little over four thousand, or more than half of the entire number of offenses in this class. In addition there are violations of city ordinances, totaling eighteen hundred, and vagrancy, over two hundred, which added to the first three major classes of offenses constitute almost six thousand out of the seven thousand offenses against public policy, leaving about twelve hundred distributed among forty-one items of a varied character.

It is seen, then, that the offenses committed most frequently by both races are gaming, lottery playing, vagrancy, drunkenness, traffic violations, liquor law violations, and the breaking of city ordinances. And the questions of their social significance and their relation to public welfare are interesting aspects of the intermingling of cultures often observed in connection with migration. Inevitably, not merely the bare statistics but the human history and folkways of the people concerned must be considered.

GENERAL CONCLUSIONS

A review of the evidence which has just been given is suggestive of certain interesting conclusions in the field of so-called race contact. Whatever one might expect to find, it is clear so far that there is nothing in the Oriental crime record indicating some special variety of crime which characterizes either the Chinese or the Japanese as racial stocks; nor is there any ground upon which to erect a theory of inborn racial tendency toward types of criminal behavior. Instead, the evidence points clearly to the fact that we have here an interesting example of certain aspects of culture mingling. The problem of adjustment of one culture to another inevitably illustrates the difficulties which arise through misunderstanding, and through the differences in the weight of emphasis which different forms of behavior are given in one culture as compared with another. It is well to understand that both custom and law as affecting human conduct belong, in each case, to a cultural unit or whole, and criminal conduct itself must be studied in relation to the cultural background of the offender. And it is equally evident that the sheer inability of newcomers as strangers in a strange world involves a temporary inability to understand and appreciate the ways and sentiments and attitudes of the life which they have entered. Much of what constitutes the criminal record of the Oriental in California is to be understood only in relation to these facts. Of those major acts which are punished as seriously harmful in the codes of most developed cultures, neither the Chinese nor the Japanese in California present a record which is excessive or which marks these groups as peculiarly dangerous to life, morals, or property. On the contrary, during a period of a quarter of a century, approximately five-sixths of the offenses committed by them are not such as involve injury to life or property, but are violations of ordinances or statutes of what may be considered relatively minor significance. It is at least fair to assume that a considerable percentage of Oriental offenses are such as express the difficulties of understanding which always characterize immigrant life in process of adjustment.

That those offenses which are in their nature seriously anti-social form a small number and percentage of the total offenses committed by the Chinese and Japanese is seen from the following table which shows the distribution of offenses according to the Penal Code classification.

TABLE 49

DISTRIBUTION OF ORIENTAL OFFENSES ACCORDING TO THE
PENAL CODE CLASSIFICATION

Classification	Chinese		Japanese		Total Orientals	
	Number	Percent-age	Number	Percent-age	Number	Percent-age
I. Offenses against the person....	671	1.03	393	2.30	1,064	1.30
IV. Offenses against property......	626	0.96	632	3.70	1,258	1.53
II.–IV. Offenses against public policy, morals, public health and safety	63,688	98.00	16,078	94.01	79,766	97.17
Total	64,985	100.00	17,103	100.00	82,088	100.00

The results show that among the Chinese, out of a total of approximately sixty-five thousand arrests, those of a violent character and dangerous to human life form slightly over 1 per cent; and offenses that would be harmful to property and are committed for the purpose of gain constitute less than 1 per cent of the total.

For the Japanese, out of a total of over seventeen thousand offenses, those of a violent and dangerous character form 2.30 per cent, and those of a predatory character form 3.70 per cent of the total.

Averaging these offenses as an Oriental total, offenses of violence, depicting a destructive attitude toward others, form 1.3 per cent; and offenses against property form approximately 1.5 per cent of the total number.

The bulk of offenses committed by each group lie in the class called "Public Policy": out of their total of 64,985 offenses the Chinese have 63,688 offenses against public policy; and out of a total of 17,103 the Japanese have 16,078 such offenses. These figures constitute for the Chinese 98.0 and for the Japanese 94.01 per cent of their totals.

ANALYSIS OF ORIENTAL OFFENSES AGAINST PUBLIC POLICY

The types of offenses contained in this classification have been given in detailed tables above. From these it is seen that there is, for either race, a distinct set of offenses which is responsible for this proportionately larger number of their arrests.

It is of value, in order to ascertain the social significance of these offenses, to examine closely their contents and nature. In this way also may perhaps be traced what mental attitude underlies their perpetration.

CHINESE OFFENSES

Among the Chinese the offenses given in their order in Table 50 (p. 66) are responsible for the major proportion of arrests in this category.

Lottery.—Lottery playing is the offense for which in every locality the largest number of Chinese arrests occur. Taken together with gaming and narcotics almost 80 per cent of Chinese offenses are accounted for. Here is not only an interesting illustration of what seem to be certain cultural habits of the Chinese people, but also an illustration of certain results of the segregation of aliens as both a policy and a fact. Leading students[1] have called attention to certain differences between the behavior of the Chinese in America and that of the Japanese. In the long period of their

---

[1] Notably R. D. McKenzie, in *Oriental Exclusion* (Chicago, University of Chicago Press, 1928).

residence here, the Chinese have become thoroughly segregated both in residence and in occupations. They have yielded to American social pressure and have gradually come to live and to carry on business in special sections of our cities; and they have tended to avoid occupations which bring them into competition with whites. To some extent the very offenses

TABLE 50

CHINESE OFFENSES AGAINST PUBLIC POLICY LEADING TO
HIGH FREQUENCY OF ARRESTS, ACCORDING TO
CALIFORNIA POLICE RECORDS,
1900–1927

Class of Crime	Number	Percentage
Lottery	28,670	44.12
Gaming	14,855	22.86
Narcotics	7,635	11.75
Vagrancy	3,359	5.17
Miscellaneous city ordinances	3,087	4.75
Immigration laws	1,605	2.47
Traffic laws	681	1.05
Disturbing the peace	281	0.43
Prostitution	230	0.35
Drunkenness	213	0.33
Carrying concealed weapons	185	0.29
Medical treatment	169	0.26
State medical laws	163	0.25
Total	61,133	94.05

which often land them in prison constitute more or less tolerated occupations which the native white considers characteristic of the Chinese. This very situation not only has tended to continue these characteristic Chinese offenses longer than would ordinarily have been the case if segregation in occupations had not been forced upon them, but it has probably increased their number. Ordinarily it seems probable that these offenses would have gradually decreased and become insignificant as Chinese crimes if the segregation process had not created an abnormal situation. To the Chinese, lotteries and gambling are occupations sanctioned by their own customs; these are not sanctioned by American ideas but the Chinese have not been encouraged to develop an appreciation of these ideas and of their values. Moreover, as occupations, even in spite of being illegal and subject to punishment, they are probably as safe for the Chinese as many legal occupations in which they must become competitors with white workers and so run the risk of ill treatment such as has characterized so much of Chinese history in California.

Because the Chinese are so thoroughly segregated they tend to supply to their own community those recreational and amusement activities to which they are accustomed and in doing so to conform to their own code rather than to ours.[1] Lottery playing with the Chinese is a lifetime habit; a lottery ticket is purchased by old and young in the old country as an American is wont to buy a ticket to the theater. Here in this country they ply their lottery activities among themselves, quietly, without any wish (outside of the knowledge that it is against the law) to do any social harm thereby.

Gambling.—Next to lotteries, gambling is the most serious offense among California Orientals, occasioning a heavy volume of arrests. Out of a total of about sixty-two thousand arrests, close to fifteen thousand were for gambling.

Gaming, for intelligible reasons, is prohibited in one way or another somewhat universally. There are places where the law permits regulated gambling, as in Monte Carlo, for instance; and there are some states within the Union where divers devices are permissible for the playing of games undeniably of a gambling character, such as guessing or punching machines of various types. In California the Penal Code clearly defines gaming as a misdemeanor. Section 330, chapter x, reads:

A person who deals, plays, or carries on, opens, or causes to be opened, or who conducts either as owner or employee, whether for hire or not, any game of: Faro, monte, roulette, lansquenet, rouge-et-noir, rondo, fan, fan-tan, stud-horse poker, seven-and-a-half, twenty-one, hokey-pokey, or any banking or percentage game, played with cards, dice, or any device, for money, checks, credit or other representative of value.

And any person who plays, bets, at or against any of said prohibited games, is guilty of a misdemeanor and shall be punished by a fine of not less than $100, not more than $500, or imprisonment in the county jail for six months, or both fine and imprisonment.

Section 330a prohibits gambling by slot machine; Sec. 331 prohibits gambling in houses owned or rented; Sec. 332 prohibits "winning by fraudulent means—sleight-of-hand, pretensions to fortune-telling, trick, etc."; Sec. 337a prohibits "pool-selling, bookmaking, etc."

Mainly because of the element of chance and because it is conducive to the direct and material gain of one individual by the losses of another, gambling is prohibited by law. But there is another and graver reason which has a serious bearing on the general welfare, namely, the unhealthy moral influences that surround and emanate from a gambling den. Generally these are places where vagrants and individuals of irresponsible character congregate.

---

[1] It is perhaps worth noting that it is only in recent times in our own civilization that selling lottery tickets has come to be illegal.

With reference to the Chinese in regard to gambling, the following observation made at an earlier date by the Chief of Police of Los Angeles is suggestive:

. . . . in the matter of gambling, ... it appears that the Chinese, although they gamble almost universally, gamble very mildly indeed. They play fan-tan or Pie-gow, as the Englishman plays club-rubber or whist, or Americans play bridge and poker. For years in San Francisco, while the Chinese gambling "dens" were periodically raided by the police, there were many places where poker and other games were openly played by white men in which far larger sums of money were lost, and in several of the principal saloons pools were sold on the races and prize-fights.— San Francisco is of all places the one where gambling can least appropriately be called an "Oriental" vice, since every form of it has flourished among the white population under the sufferance of municipal authority.[1]

The Chinese or Japanese themselves do not seem to regard gambling as a vice, but think of it as we do of a game of bridge for the social entertainment of friends; and there is no violence or hysteria connected with it for them. When confined to themselves, gambling is mild in degree and relatively harmless in effects, Mrs. Coolidge says, and quotes evidence from Edmund Mitchell:

It is only when the riff-raff of other races are allowed to take a hand and to utilize the Chinese tables, games and banks, for the gratification of their own propensities, that anything like widespread mischief is wrought. A Chinaman in rare instances loses his all when gaming among his own country-men; but if this result does happen, he goes next day contentedly back to work and is not, like most ruined gamblers of European stock, permanently incapacitated for honest toil.[2]

Gambling, as we term it, is for the Oriental a recreation and not primarily a feverish scramble for wealth. There are undoubtedly what we know as professional gamblers among them, but these do not account for the large numbers of arrests that figure in police records. These numbers are taken from among the work-a-day Chinamen who seek to while away a leisure hour at an accustomed game.

There is no gainsaying the presence and the evil effects of the gambling "joint" operated by Chinese owners, undoubtedly the "hang-out" for many undesirables. But these again, it is safe to say, are not so numerous or so widespread as to account for the thousands of gaming arrests; and it is a question how many of them come within the radius of police attention.

Narcotics.—The offense next in rank to gambling is that of violations of the narcotic laws. The relation of the Chinese to the opium problem is not only a troublesome one but a sad one. Their race is connected with the

---

[1] M. R. Coolidge, *Chinese Immigration* (Henry Holt & Company, New York), pp. 451–52.

[2] Coolidge, *op. cit.*, p. 452.

beginnings and the continuation of a health-breaking habit for which they are not themselves wholly responsible. The history of this problem is generally known, and equally well known is the fact that for the Chinese the opium habit is generations old. It is claimed by some observers that their way of taking opium works less havoc with their human efficiency than is known to be the case with the white man's use of this or other drugs. On this topic Mrs. Coolidge says:

> The opium habit, notwithstanding its expense, prevails among the poor as well as the rich, but it is difficult to say to what extent. Among Caucasians the taking of opium is the synonym of ruin; but if we should judge of the extent of the use of opium by the number of Chinese who are incapacitated by it, it would certainly be very small. The immigrant farmers and laborers that are found in the United States have as a class none of the characteristic symptoms of the habitual opium-taker. Either they use opium in moderation, much as the American uses tobacco, or they are less affected by it than Caucasians are. In some parts of China alcoholic stimulants are used freely by all classes but drunkenness is almost unknown.[1]

And again:

> It has already been shown that opium-taking in moderation as ordinarily practiced by them in this country, is no more disastrous than the use of tobacco among Americans; and that when carried to excess, its effects are scarcely more disastrous to society than the excessive liquor drinking which is the characteristic Caucasian vice.[2]

Undoubtedly the opium habit is health wrecking, as is any narcotic habit. The effects of narcotics are doubly pernicious, first in the creation of an unnatural craving, then in the devastating after-effects, causing a vicious circle, leading generally to the ruin or death of the victim. This, however, those people who know the Chinese temperament aver is not common among the Chinese. The almost crazed rush to use a narcotic of this nature—not for a moment of quiet recreation, as is the case with the Chinese, but to achieve a sleeping forgetfulness of self—is common with white men; and the effect of the drug on Caucasians is described as truly horrible, lacking, as they do, both taste and moderation in its use. Mr. Konrad Bercovici, a keen observer of the life among immigrant groups, describes this fact rather realistically:

> I have visited one [opium joint] several times myself, and counted eight white people out of eleven in the place; people whose names are frequently blazoned in the papers as principals of this and that. There they looked more like disemboweled creatures from whom everything that had a semblance of real life had been taken out. Their brains seemed to have been scooped out from within their skulls. Their eyes were bleary and partly closed. The twitching lips and the arms hanging over the edges of the narrow cots on which they lay down, made them a picture of contemptible

---

[1] Coolidge, *op. cit.,* p. 9.

[2] *Ibid.,* pp. 452–53.

distress portrayed to horrify. The Chinese lay in a trance without in any way giving the impression of disgust and horror given by the others.

When I asked one who knew what caused the difference of appearance between opium-smokers, I was answered: "Because the Chinese know and the white man doesn't. White man hog. He eats much. He drinks much. He smokes much."[1]

Through the yellow press a somewhat lurid picture of Chinese vice in this country has come to be accepted as fact and as typical of "Chinatown." The out-of-town sightseer takes the bus there to get a "thrill" out of seeing at first hand the "vice dens" and opium joints that he or she has read so much about. That much of this is staged, beginning with the decoy in the Chinatown bus, the visitor is not usually aware. Mr. Bercovici tells:

There are numerous places especially conducted for the special benefit of the sightseer. For a consideration, one is shown, in a room of a rear house, rows upon rows of beds on which lie the stupified opium-smokers. But most of these men and sometimes, women, are hired by the hour to simulate conditions which Mr. Poole and Mrs. Grundy are going to denounce in their home town on their return from wicked New York.[2]

In spite of these possible differences between white and Chinese use of narcotics, there is no intent here to minimize the evil of the situation. There is, however, no evident ground to ascribe the increasing use of drugs among white residents to the Chinese. Until the growth and sale of opium in its many forms is more adequately controlled internationally one may expect an increasing number of offenses on the part of both whites and Orientals in spite of the arrest and punishment of individuals.

Violations of local ordinances.—One of the serious difficulties which every immigrant faces is that of knowing or understanding the various ordinances and statutes. The large group of arrests for violations of local ordinances attests this predicament of the Chinese and also of the Japanese. A review of the nature of these—riding their bicycles on certain prohibited parts of the road, piling goods on prohibited parts of the sidewalk or gutter, crowding in a lodging house, violating the bathing, building, plumbing, park, smoke, firecracker, curfew, license, and hundreds of such ordinances —does not usually indicate on their part an intention to do harm, nor that they possess criminal tendencies. In this connection Dr. Fairchild observes in regard to European immigrants:

In the matter of crime the effort to make generalizations is complicated by the fact that it is necessary to take into account not only the number of crimes, but the nature and severity of the criminal act. Tests of criminality, to be accurate, should include quality as well as quantity. . . . . . When crime records are studied more closely

---

[1] Konrad Bercovici, *Around the World in New York* (1924), pp. 104–23.

[2] *Ibid.,* p. 108.

it becomes apparent that a large share of the offenses are violations of the city ordinances, offenses which are comparatively trivial in themselves, do not indicate any special tendency toward criminality, and are in many cases intimately associated with a low station in life. The moral character of the alien may in this way be seriously misrepresented.[1]

Moreover, it is but necessary to become familiar with the status of the Orientals in the public mind on the Pacific Coast, to learn of the deep-seated antagonism against them, in order to realize how easily a large number of charges against them accumulate. The records of other investigations involving the behavior of alien groups indicate that all such groups, including Orientals, labor under the handicap growing out of difficulties of cultural adjustment, such as language, standards of living, institutional variations, and similar conditions. The Chinese and Japanese illustrate these difficulties precisely as do other alien or immigrant groups, though it should be added in their behalf that the percentage of such offenses to the total number of offenses is greater than is indicated for white immigrant groups.[2] Or, reversing the statement, there is reason to believe that an even smaller percentage of all Oriental offenses were of the more serious sorts as compared with various alien white groups.

Vagrancy.—The term "vagrancy" is defined as "without being usefully employed or showing that there is possession of or attachment to useful employment." The arrests for vagrancy as here included are, however, not to be construed as indicating such numbers of unemployed, shiftless Chinese. In this case a charge of vagrancy is preferred against anyone found in a place where a gambling game is going on. When a raid is made on a gambling place, everyone found on the premises is arrested; the players and the proprietor (or conductor of the game) are indicted for gambling, while the lookers-on, including everyone found in the vicinity, are charged with vagrancy. The same is true with respect to a raid made on a house suspected of being disreputable or where there may be opium-smoking.

Violations of immigration laws.—With respect to the violation of immigration laws, the gravity of the offense can be adjudged from certain knowledge of two things: first, the nature of this violation; and, second, by comparing the behavior of other immigrant groups in this direction. However, available data for such a comparison is lacking. Generally, this offense consists of smuggling in a fellow-countryman from the border

---

[1] Henry Pratt Fairchild, *Immigration,* The Macmillan Co., New York, 1925, pp. 329–30.

[2] Compare the findings of the Immigration Commission, Vol. II, p. 198, in which the record of the Chicago police arrests for four years (1905–1908) shows that 75.2 per cent of all arrests were for offenses against public policy.

countries. Within about a quarter of a century the Chinese had 1,605 arrests on this charge, constituting 2.47 per cent of the total number of their arrests.

Violations of traffic laws.—This type of offense requires almost no explanation. It is shared, in various degrees and quantities, by all vehicle owners and drivers. The relatively small number of arrests for this offense among the Chinese may perhaps be explained by the fact that they are either more careful drivers, or that there are fewer vehicle owners and drivers among them.

Disturbing the peace.—Two hundred and eighty-one arrests for this cause out of approximately sixty-five thousand arrests is not a number by which to decide that the Chinese are noisy, quarrelsome people. On the contrary it is a factual indication that they are a peace-loving, unassuming, modest people.

Prostitution.—Neither can the charge of gross immorality be preferred against them when it is seen that in the course of over twenty years, from all over the state, out of a total of approximately sixty-five thousand arrests, only two hundred and thirty were for immoral practices. In spite of a popular belief to the contrary, this is in line with the observed rather high standard of sex morals which observers of Chinese life report.

Sexual morality in the villages [Chinese] is very high, prostitution and illegitimacy occurring only rarely. The restraints upon women, the very early and almost universal marriage, the strength of the family ties, and, among the middle and higher classes, the system of concubinage all combine to produce a very high standard of moral restraint. Prostitution exists in all the cities and especially in the river and sea-board towns where single men congregate, but its extent is small as compared with the great cities of Europe and America. . . . . Arthur Smith declares that: "Chinese morality at its best is fully equal to that of any Western land"; and if other modern writers may be believed, he might have said with truth that at its worst, it is no worse.[1]

Drunkenness.—Mrs. Coolidge says: "In some parts of China alcoholic stimulants are used freely by all classes but drunkenness is almost unknown," and this observation seems to be borne out by the records of drunkenness of the Chinese here. There were 213 arrests for drunkenness out of a total of 64,985 arrests.

Carrying concealed weapons.—Relatively, 185 arrests for this offense over two decades is an inconspicuous number, but, unfortunately, the mention of "concealed weapons" in connection with the Chinese brings immediately to mind their tongs and tong wars, by which the average reader of our newspapers inclines to regard any and every Chinaman as a "killer" or as having some stealthy, secret connection with one.

---

[1] Cf. M. R. Coolidge, *Chinese Immigration*, pp. 9–10.

It is impossible to estimate the significance of "tongs" in regard to the Chinese record of crime until a better knowledge of these organizations is made public. A trustworthy description of tong organization and activity remains to be written.[1] Such knowledge as is available, however, indicates that the activities of these organizations are an outgrowth of the peculiar position of the Chinese in California. They are organizations of a somewhat inevitable sort where distinct and conflicting cultures meet and where through failure of understanding the newcomers find the need of self-protection. The assumption on the part of the Chinese that through their own organizations they might control the behavior of their members without recourse to the American police and courts easily became the basis of misunderstanding and suspicion. And their existence and evident activities, which grew out of their segregated life, have tended to aggravate and perpetuate the segregation itself. Undoubtedly at times the tongs have been the instruments or agencies of considerable violence, though it has always been easy to exaggerate this fact. At the present time, with the decreasing numbers and importance of the Chinese in California, tongs seem to be a waning influence.

JAPANESE OFFENSES

The Japanese in California have been increasing in numbers steadily, from ten and one-half thousand in 1900 to almost seventy-two thousand in 1920. During this time there were about nineteen thousand arrests out of a total for all groups of offenders of over two million arrests.

Certain characteristics of their offenses may be briefly commented upon. There is a general resemblance to the Chinese as regards offenses: out of nineteen thousand arrests more than thirteen thousand, or 77.58 per cent, were for offenses classed as against public policy. The trend of offenses is, however, in one respect more nearly parallel to that of native or alien white groups, in that only 3.08 per cent of arrests are for offenses against the lottery laws, as compared with 44.12 per cent for the Chinese. While the Japanese indulge in gambling considerably, their arrests for this offense do not reach so high a percentage as for the Chinese, being 15.78 per cent, as against 22.86 per cent for the Chinese. Unlike the Chinese, the Japanese do not seem to indulge greatly in opium-smoking, the volume of their arrests for violation of the narcotics laws being very small (less than 1 per cent). On the other hand, they incline more than the Chinese to the white man's indulgence in alcoholic liquors. Arrests for drunkenness and violation of liquor laws together constitute a higher percentage of their total

---

[1] My colleague, Dr. C. N. Reynolds, is now engaged upon such a study, which it is hoped will appear in due time.

arrests than do arrests for violation of the opium and narcotic laws among the Chinese (16.92 per cent as compared to 11.75 per cent).

TABLE 51

JAPANESE OFFENSES AGAINST PUBLIC POLICY LEADING TO
HIGH FREQUENCY OF ARRESTS ACCORDING TO
CALIFORNIA POLICE RECORDS, 1900–1927

Class of Offenses	Number	Percentage
Traffic regulations violations.........	4,540	26.55
Miscellaneous city ordinances........	1,825	10.67
Gambling	2,669	15.78
Drunkenness	1,853	10.83
Liquor laws violations...............	1,041	6.09
Lottery violations...................	527	3.08
Vagrancy	263	1.54
Disturbing the peace...............	234	1.37
Immigration laws violations..........	149	0.87
Opium and narcotics violations......	137	0.80
Total	13,238	77.58

On the whole, the Japanese are less segregated in residence, occupations, and other respects than the Chinese, and this is reflected in their relatively lower criminal record, as measured by offenses characteristic of traits of a segregated group.

The following table, employing the classification of the Immigration Commission's study, gives a picture of the variety of Japanese arrests in nineteen important centers in California, and also the prison commitments to the state prison at San Quentin.

On the whole, the record of the Japanese in California is clearly that of an orderly and industrious people, obedient to the laws of the state. And except for a few types of offenses the same is true of the Chinese.

Bureau of the Census report on "Prisoners in 1923."—The following excerpts from the report of the Bureau of the Census shows the relatively unimportant position held by the Chinese and Japanese in the commitment of crime in the country. The report gives data concerning the numbers of prisoners as found on January 1, 1923, and committed between January 1 and June 30, 1923, to prisons and reformatories, jails and workhouses, throughout the country.[1]

---

[1] *Prisoners in 1923*, Bureau of the Census Publication, 1926.

TABLE 52

Number and Percentage of Japanese Offenses According to Immigration Commission Classification, Police Records in 19 Centers in California, and San Quentin Prison Records, 1900–1927

Place	Gainful Offenses		Violent Offenses		Public Policy Offenses		Chastity Offenses		Unclassified Offenses	
	Number	Percentage	Number	Percentage	Number	Percentage	Number	Percentage	Number	Percentage
San Francisco	70	4.4	32	2.0	1,409	89.0	50	3.2	22	1.4
Los Angeles	138	1.3	191	1.9	9,305	90.6	20	0.2	620	6.0
Oakland	23	1.5	49	3.1	1,478	94.0	..	...	22	1.4
San Jose	6	2.7	10	4.6	194	89.0	..	...	8	3.7
Sacramento (city)	14	3.1	70	15.4	360	79.1	..	...	11	2.4
Stockton	2	2.0	..	...	100	98.0	..		..	...
Berkeley	11	5.5	4	2.0	79	89.5	..	...	6	3.0
Santa Barbara (city)....	1	1.0	1	1.0	98	96.0	..	...	2	2.0
Fresno County	24	4.4	20	3.7	1,482	88.2	..	...	20	3.7
Sacramento County	18	13.5	10	7.5	70	52.7	..	...	35	26.3
Santa Clara County.....	10	22.7	6	13.6	18	41.0	..	...	10	22.7
San Joaquin County.....	4	14.3	2	7.1	21	75.0	..	...	1	3.6
Alameda County	9	19.1	9	19.1	29	61.8	..	...	..	...
Imperial County	15	6.2	10	4.1	202	83.5	..	...	15	6.2
Kern County	2	7.1	4	14.3	18	64.3	..	...	4	14.3
San Benito County......	1	7.7	..	...	11	84.6	..	...	1	7.7
Sutter County	2	16.7	1	8.3	9	75.0	..	...	..	...
Monterey County	3	14.3	7	33.4	10	47.6	..	...	1	4.7
San Mateo County......	..	...	..	...	1	14.3	..	...	6	85.7
San Quentin Prison.....	65	43.9	76	51.4	1	0.7	4	2.7	2	1.3

Table 53 (p. 76) gives the numerical distribution of prisoners found and committed to such institutions in 1923.

On January 1, 1923, there were found in two main classes of prison institutions in the country, 368 Chinese and Japanese: 257 in prisons and reformatories, and 111 in jails and workhouses, while there were about 15,000 other foreign-born groups, 34,178 Negroes, and 58,238 native-born whites. The Indians, numbering 413, and unknown races, numbering 526, join the Chinese and Japanese in the minority group.

The report makes comparison of the population in these institutions and the general population, eighteen years and over, in the country in 1920, bringing out in this way the position of each group with respect to the population in the country and the population found in each institution and the numbers committed thereto. Table 54 (p. 76)[1] is included for purposes of comparison, but without comment.

---

[1] *Prisoners in 1923*, Table 30, p. 60.

TABLE 53

NUMERICAL DISTRIBUTION BY COLOR, RACE, AND NATIVITY, OF PRISONERS
IN 1923, PRESENT AND COMMITTED*

Nativity, Color, Race	Present, January 1, 1923			Committed, January–June, 1923		
	Total	Prisons and Reformatories	Jails and Workhouses	Total	Prisons and Reformatories	Jails and Workhouses
All classes	109,075	80,935	28,140	166,356	19,080	147,276
Whites	73,549	54,787	18,762	124,172	14,164	110,008
Native-born	58,238	44,790	13,448	90,496	11,825	78,671
Foreign-born	15,061	9,931	5,130	31,054	2,297	28,757
Unknown	250	66	184	2,622	42	2,580
Negroes	34,178	25,243	8,935	38,821	4,581	34,240
Chinese and Japanese......	368	257	111	441	105	336
Indians	413	344	69	835	104	731
Other races	41	31	10	54	11	43
Unknown races	526	273	253	2,033	115	1,918

* *Prisoners in 1923*, Bureau of the Census Publication, 1926, p. 58, Table 29 (abridged).

TABLE 54

PERCENTAGE OF DISTRIBUTION, BY COLOR, RACE, AND NATIVITY, OF PRISONERS
IN 1923, PRESENT AND COMMITTED

Nativity, Color, Race	Population Eighteen Years and Over	Prisoners Present			Prisoners Committed		
		Total	Prisons and Reformatories	Jails and Workhouses	Total	Prisons and Reformatories	Jails and Workhouses
All classes	100.0	100.0	100.0	100.0	100.0	100.0	100.0
Whites	90.3	67.4	67.7	66.7	74.6	74.2	74.7
Native-born	70.9	53.4	55.3	47.8	54.4	62.0	53.4
Foreign-born	19.4	13.8	12.3	18.2	18.7	12.0	19.5
Unknown	...	0.2	0.1	0.7	1.6	0.2	1.8
Negro	9.3	31.3	31.2	31.8	23.3	24.0	23.2
Indian	0.2	0.4	0.4	0.2	0.5	0.5	0.5
Chinese and Japanese..	0.2	0.3	0.3	0.4	0.3	0.6	0.2
Other races	...*	...*	...*	...*	...*	0.1	...*
Races unknown	...	0.5	0.3	0.9	1.2	0.6	1.3

* Less than one-tenth of one per cent.

V. OCCUPATIONS OF ORIENTAL DELINQUENTS

In assembling the arrest data an endeavor was made to obtain details regarding the occupation of the offender as given at the time of arrest. This information aids in an interpretation of the character of the Oriental offenders. It may give some clue as to the prevalence of shiftlessness, idleness, and vagrancy among them and may also indicate to some extent the number of professional gamblers and other individuals with socially undesirable occupations.

The occupations of 12,501 Chinese and 13,661 Japanese offenders were ascertained from the police day-books in the various localities in the state. In the table below is given the list of their occupations in alphabetical order.

TABLE 55

OCCUPATIONS OF CHINESE AND JAPANESE ARRESTED IN 26 LOCALITIES
IN CALIFORNIA, 1900–1927

Occupation	Number		Occupation	Number	
	Chinese	Japanese		Chinese	Japanese
Acrobat	3	..	Car washer	3	1
Actor	34	14	Carpenter	14	27
Actress	1	3	Cashier	3	3
Advertising man	3	1	Chair-maker	3	..
Agent	26	37	Chauffeur	30	412
Apprentice	1	..	Checker	..	1
Artist	2	9	Chemist	1	2
Attorney	1	9	Cigar-maker	14	14
Auctioneer	2	..	Circus-man	..	1
Aviator	1	3	Cleaner	66	48
			Clerk	409	61
Banker	..	2	Cobbler	1	..
Barber	32	89	Collector	1	1
Bathhouse keeper	1	3	Contractor	4	10
Bell-boy	11	19	Cook	851	951
Blacksmith	..	5	Costumer	..	1
Boat-builder	..	8			
Bookkeeper	42	17	Dairyman	1	23
Box-maker	1	..	Dancer	..	1
Broker	3	32	Dancing teacher	..	1
Builder	1	1	Decorator	5	3
Butcher	57	7	Delivery boy	1	3
Butler	1	4	Dentist	1	18
Buyer	2	2	Designer	..	1
			Director	..	1
Candy-maker	..	12	Dishwasher	34	38
Cannery-worker	9	13			

TABLE 55 (*Continued*)

Occupation	Number		Occupation	Number	
	Chinese	Japanese		Chinese	Japanese
Doctor	33	65	Jeweler	2	12
Domestic	59	136	Joss-house keeper	1	..
Draftsman	1	..			
Driver	86	434	Laborer	4,497	3,451
Druggist	24	20	Landlord	76	63
Dye-worker	..	27	Laundryman	856	207
			Leather-worker	..	1
Editor	..	9	Longshoreman	..	2
Electrician	2	8	Lottery-agent	131	13
Elevator boy	..	9	Lottery-keeper	31	1
Employment agent	..	3	Lumberman	..	1
Engineer	..	6			
Entertainer	..	3	Manager	13	27
Exporter	..	1	Manufacturer	6	12
			Marker	2	..
Farmer	143	1,138	Mattress-maker	..	1
Fertilizer	..	2	Masseur	..	7
Fireman	1	2	Mechanic	21	74
Fisherman	43	362	Merchant	2,672	1,398
Florist	3	141	Midwife	..	4
Foreman	1	2	Milkman	..	1
Fortune-teller	..	2	Miner	5	1
Furnisher	..	1	Minister	1	24
			Missionary	..	1
Gambler	131	19	Movieman	3	5
Game-keeper	3	2	Moving-picture operator	..	1
Gardener	35	835	Musician	4	4
Garage-man	2	40			
Garbage-man	..	16	Naval officer	..	1
Gas-station keeper	1	1	Newsboy	5	2
Grocer	35	79	Newspaperman	..	12
			Noodle-maker	..	5
Hatchery	..	1	Nurse	..	1
Hat-maker	..	1	Nurseryman	2	143
Herbalist	54	1			
Highbinder	8	..	Office boy	1	2
Hobo	18	2	Officer (society)	1	..
Hophead	19	..	Oil worker	..	3
Hop-joint keeper	2	..	Orchardist	..	1
Hop-peddler	32	..			
Hotel-keeper	6	137	Packer	8	16
Hotel-worker	1	1	Painter	7	14
Housewife	74	251	Pantryman	1	10
			Paper merchant	..	1
Inspector	2	1	Peddler	373	198
Insurance-man	1	30	Pharmacist	..	3
Interpreter	21	45	Photographer	1	21
Iron-worker	2	..	Pimp	4	..
Janitor	26	155	Plasterer	1	1

TABLE 55 (*Concluded*)

Occupation	Number		Occupation	Number	
	Chinese	Japanese		Chinese	Japanese
Plumber	1	24	Soda-fountain employee.	..	4
Poolroom	4	56	Soldier	1	2
Porter	31	181	Stable-boss	..	2
Presser	..	1	Steward	4	2
Printer	3	28	Student	185	245
Prize-fighter	..	2			
Promoter	..	2	Tailor	49	54
Proprietor	3	3	Tanner	..	1
Prostitute	11	..	Teacher	1	7
Publisher	..	10	Telegrapher	1	..
			Theater proprietor	2	5
Rancher	35	420	Tong-leader	5	..
Real estate agent	..	13	Tourist	1	2
Religious worker	..	1	Trainer	..	1
Repairer	..	3	Translator	3	..
Reporter	1	5	Trucking	..	3
Restaurant keeper	360	388			
Retired	65	7	Upholsterer	1	..
Ring-house keeper	..	29			
Rooming house keeper	4	30	Valet	..	1
			Veterinary	..	2
Sailor	13	6	Waiter	351	225
Salesman	67	174	Waitress	..	19
Saloon-keeper	2	..	Watchmaker	..	1
Seaman	6	..	Watchman	4	3
Seamstress	3	1	Wash-house keeper	..	1
Secretary	..	5	Window-washer	..	2
Seedman	..	3	Wiper	3	1
Ship-captain	..	1	Yardman	..	1
Shipper	..	3			
Shoe-maker	6	19			
Showman	..	1	Totals	12,496	13,645

It will be seen that, as has been said, the arrests were made among Orientals engaged in almost every occupation ordinarily known and current among the every-day, work-a-day population. It is suggested, however, that there are several occupations in which both races predominate, some in which the Chinese are more numerously engaged, and some which have become predominantly a Japanese avocation. That this is the case is shown in Table 56.

The commonest occupation among offenders of both races is that of laborer: there were 4,497 Chinese and 3,451 Japanese laborers arrested. Following, is that of merchant: there were 2,672 Chinese and 1,398 Japanese merchants arrested. The third in rank common to both is that of cook; the fourth is restaurant-keeping; and the fifth, student. A large number of arrests are about equally divided among these occupations.

TABLE 56

NUMBER AND PERCENTAGE OF ARRESTS IN TYPICAL ORIENTAL
OCCUPATIONS, ACCORDING TO CALIFORNIA
POLICE DEPARTMENT RECORDS

Occupation	Chinese		Japanese	
	Number	Percentage	Number	Percentage
Laborer	4,497	35.9	3,451	25.3
Merchant	2,672	21.4	1,398	10.2
Cook	851	6.8	951	7.0
Farmer	143	1.1	1,138	8.3
Clerk	409	3.3	61	0.4
Chauffeur	30	0.2	412	3.0
Driver	86	0.7	434	3.2
Laundry	856	6.8	207	1.5
Restaurant-keeper	360	2.9	388	2.8
Peddler	373	3.0	198	1.5
Rancher	35	0.3	420	3.1
Gardener	35	0.3	835	6.1
Fisherman	43	0.3	362	2.7
Florist	3	0.0	141	1.0
Nurseryman	2	0.0	143	1.0
Student	185	1.5	245	1.8
Salesman	67	0.5	174	1.3
Porter	31	0.3	181	1.3
Janitor	26	0.2	155	1.1
Hotel-keeper	6	0.0	137	1.0
Domestic	59	0.5	136	1.0
Housewife	74	0.6	251	1.8
Barber	32	0.3	89	0.7
Total	10,875	...	11,907	...

There seem to be, however, some occupations in which the Chinese offenders are more numerous, for example: laundryman, 856 Chinese compared to 207 Japanese; peddler, 373 Chinese and 198 Japanese; clerking, 409 Chinese and 61 Japanese. Those in which the Japanese seem to predominate are: farmer, 1,138 Japanese as against 143 Chinese; chauffeur, 412 Japanese to 30 Chinese; driver, 434 Japanese to 86 Chinese; rancher, 420 Japanese to 35 Chinese; gardening, 835 Japanese to 35 Chinese; fishing, 362 Japanese to 43 Chinese; nurseryman and florist, 284 Japanese to 5 Chinese; salesman, 174 Japanese to 67 Chinese; porter and janitor,

336 Japanese to 57 Chinese; hotel-keeper, 137 Japanese to 6 Chinese; domestic worker, 136 Japanese to 59 Chinese.[1]

The occupation of housewife was recorded for Japanese women arrested mostly for violation of the Wright Act; Chinese women were arrested for lottery-ticket possession, and Wright Act violation.

As a check, it is of interest to compare these occupation data of criminals with the census of all Oriental occupations in California. The distribution of all Orientals among the occupational classes in California is as follows:

TABLE 57

PERCENTAGE DISTRIBUTION OF MALE ORIENTALS AMONG
OCCUPATIONAL CLASSES, 1920[2]

Class of Occupation	Total Number for State	Total Oriental	Percentage of Oriental Total
Agricultural husbandry	262,982	29,660	49.2
Extraction of minerals	24,620	416	0.7
Manufacturing and mechanical industries	389,013	5,773	9.6
Transportation	115,159	1,698	2.8
Trade	173,431	7,368	12.2
Public service	44,383	474	0.8
Professional service	64,901	833	1.4
Domestic and personal service	78,432	13,146	21.7
Clerical service	73,192	816	1.4
Total	1,226,113	60,294	99.8

The occupational distribution of the Chinese and Japanese as found in the police records is in keeping with the total occupational distribution of Orientals in California. The majority are in agriculture, in which class are contained the large numbers of laborers on farms and gardens; followed by domestic and personal service, in which class are cooks, waiters, laundry-workers, janitors, and others. In trade the majority are merchants and clerks in stores, followed by laborers and miscellaneous workers in manufacturing and mechanical industries.

The foregoing tabulation shows the distribution of the male population among selected industries current in the state. The employed Oriental

---

[1] Occupational names are given as recorded, though probably at times different terms are used for the same occupation, as for example, "farmer" and "rancher."

[2] In the construction of this and similar tables involving comparison between total California population figures and those found for Orientals in this research, the *United States Census,* 1920, Vol. IV, Occupations (pp. 343–51) was used.

population represent 87.7 per cent of their male population; and employed as a whole for the state represent 64.12 per cent of the male population in the state.

It is safe to say that these data on their employment furnish indirect confirmation of the earlier statement that the large percentage of Oriental arrests are for offenses against "public policy": that is to say, that the arrests made among them do not indicate a particularly vicious population. This fact is further suggested by the very small number of seriously criminal acts, such as murder, robbery, burglary, forgery, conspiracy, and the like, committed by them. "It is," as Mrs. Coolidge asserts, "an impossibility for any race to be extremely industrious and at the same time highly immoral, intemperate and criminal . . . . and it has been universally granted that the Chinese are the most industrious of peoples."[1] This is equally true of the Japanese. Their trained hardihood, patience, and endurance to work long intense hours on the land tends to preclude for them, because of sheer lack of idle time, the possibility of participating in criminal activities. And as Boddy suggests: "If the natural bent of the Japanese immigrant could be followed without interference, 95 per cent of them would unquestionably go into farming, and for this reason they do not contribute to city congestion and its attendant evils."[2]

---

[1] Coolidge, op. cit., p. 452.

[2] E. M. Boddy, The Japanese in America, p. 25. (Privately printed, Los Angeles, 1921.)

VI. AGES OF ORIENTAL OFFENDERS

It was possible to secure information on the ages of 17,509 Chinese and 12,949 Japanese, as given at the time of their arrest. The following table gives the numbers arrested within each group.

TABLE 58

AGES OF ORIENTAL OFFENDERS, ACCORDING TO CALIFORNIA
POLICE RECORDS OF ARRESTS, 1900–1927

Age Group	Chinese		Japanese	
	Number	Percentage	Number	Percentage
15–19 years	470	2.68	312	2.41
20–24 years	1,968	11.24	1,150	8.88
25–29 years	2,454	14.01	2,135	16.48
30–34 years	2,246	12.82	2,618	20.21
35–39 years	1,588	9.07	2,779	21.45
40–44 years	1,645	9.40	2,111	16.30
45–49 years	1,513	8.64	956	7.38
50–54 years	1,728	9.87	515	3.98
55–59 years	1,219	6.96	211	1.63
60–64 years	1,364	7.79	121	0.93
65–69 years	650	3.71	31	0.24
70–74 years	378	2.16	13	0.10
75–79 years	216	1.23	1	0.01
80–84 years	49	0.28	1	0.01
85–89 years	13	0.07	...	....
90–94 years	3	0.02	...	....
95–99 years	2	0.01	...	....
100 years	2	0.01	...	....
105 years	1	0.01	...	....
Total	17,509	99.99	12,954	100.01

The numbers arrested begin to decrease in the older age groups, but more so among the Japanese than the Chinese. The majority of the Japanese arrests were drawn from among the younger age groups, 20–44, and arrests begin precipitately to decline thereafter. The bulk of the Chinese arrests are from among the age groups 20–64, and begin to decline rapidly only after the 60–64 group. Thus 83.32 per cent of the Japanese arrests were made of offenders of the ages between 20 and 44 years; but 89.80 per cent of the Chinese arrests come from offenders ranging in age between 20 and 64. Of old people, those of 65 years and over, the Japanese have but few arrests, while the Chinese count 7.52 per cent of such among their arrests. Remembering that the bulk of the Japanese arrests were made for violations of traffic rules and drunkenness, and that the majority of the Chinese were arrested for lottery playing, gambling, and opium offenses, this divergence in their age groups is understood. Furthermore, it should be kept in mind that the Chinese population at the present time is composed more largely of an older element, while that of the Japanese is younger.

It is an interesting question, though one difficult to answer quite accurately, whether the older or the younger people among the Chinese and Japanese have more frequent arrests. The following tables, separating the arrests made in each age group, from 1914 to 1927, among each race, may help to give some indication.

TABLE 59

FREQUENCY OF YEARLY ARRESTS AMONG JAPANESE BY AGE GROUPS, ACCORDING TO CALIFORNIA POLICE RECORDS OF ARRESTS, 1914–1927

Year	15–19	20–24	25–29	30–34	35–39	40–44	45–49	50–54	55–59	60–64	65–69	70–74	75–79
1914	16	85	250	182	107	53	25	7	4	3	2	1	..
1915	8	65	155	117	98	67	32	14	2	2	1	..	..
1916	12	74	253	259	147	91	56	23	8	4	5	1	1
1917	25	63	200	246	218	105	48	20	13	7	4	2	..
1918	37	91	179	293	300	164	70	32	12	4	2	..	..
1919	35	121	132	441	345	179	77	31	9	5	2	..	..
1920	26	119	144	276	250	195	66	34	12	17	3	1	1
1921	21	47	69	87	126	109	34	17	12	2	..	..	..
1922	16	64	87	115	137	136	64	15	9	7	..	1	..
1923	13	76	87	121	176	167	68	47	16	4	..	3	..
1924	18	79	96	106	211	173	104	56	24	17	3	4	..
1925	21	62	85	88	154	140	117	48	15	13	2	1	..
1926	20	83	130	107	172	159	125	66	24	17	8	2	..
1927	29	113	214	176	248	282	263	112	53	26	2	3	..

It is of interest to note that there is a higher frequency of arrests in the more advanced age groups each year, at a quite steady rate, than is the case among the younger groups, with the exception of the years 1918 and 1919; for these two years only there is a marked increase and thereafter comes a decrease.

The age group 15–19 does not show any marked increase between 1914, when there were 16 arrests, and 1927, when there were 29 arrests. The age group 20–24 shows only a slight increase from 85 arrests in 1914 to 113 in 1927. The age group 25–29 shows a decrease from 250 arrests in 1914 to 214 arrests in 1927. The age group 30–34 shows a decrease from 182 to 176. The arrests each year among these groups show a slight up-and-down movement, the highest point being reached in the years 1918 and 1919, thus: in the age group 15–19 years the frequencies of arrests from 1914 to 1919 were: 16 in 1914; 8 in 1915; 12 in 1916; 25 in 1917; 37 in 1918; and 35 in 1919. The arrests in the age group 20–24 were: 85 in 1914; 65 in 1915; 74 in 1916; 63 in 1917; 91 in 1918; and 121 in 1919. In the age group 25–29, there were 250 arrests in 1914; 155 in 1915; 253 in 1916; 200 in 1917; 179 in 1918; and 182 in 1919; in this group there is an almost steady decrease in the number of arrests each year. In the group 30–34, there were: 182 arrests in 1914; 117 in 1915; 259 in 1916; 246 in 1917; 293 in 1918; and 441 in 1919. The highest frequency of arrests occurs in this group in 1919.

After 1919 in each of these younger age groups (15–34) the frequency of arrests decreases; from which it seems quite evident that at present there seems to be no marked tendency toward lawbreaking on the part of the young Japanese. But beginning with the group 35–39, there is in each following age group a decided increase each year in the frequency of arrests. For example, in the group 35–39, arrests increased from 107 in 1914 to 248 in 1927; in the age group 40–44, arrests increased from 53 to 282; and in the age group 45–49, the increase was from 25 to 263.

From the foregoing this fact seems to stand out: Remembering that the majority of Japanese arrests are occasioned by violations of traffic laws, city ordinances, and gambling, it is evident that these offenses are committed more frequently by the older Japanese for whom it is difficult quickly to become versed sufficiently in new ways and to break with established customs. The younger people, who more readily become conversant with our laws and customs, have fewer arrests year by year, the entire arrests for the group between the ages 15–29 constituting less than one-third of the total number of arrests of those giving age data. It should be remarked also that the lowest number of arrests is in the 15–19-year-old group, testifying to the very small amount of juvenile delinquency among the Japanese. Among the 20–24-year-old group, arrests constituted 9.2 per cent of the total, which numbered almost thirteen thousand; the 25–29-year-old group constituted 16.5 per cent of the total.

On examining the ages of the Chinese offenders, two things should be borne in mind: (1) their major offenses, lottery, gambling, opium, city ordinances; and (2) the composition of their population, a majority being of the older ages with a minority of youth in this country; also the smaller number of their women.

The following table shows the frequency of arrests each year among the various age groups:

TABLE 60

FREQUENCY OF YEARLY ARRESTS AMONG CHINESE BY AGE GROUPS, ACCORDING TO
CALIFORNIA POLICE RECORDS OF ARRESTS, 1914-1927

Year	15–19	20–24	25–29	30–34	35–39	40–44	45–49	50–54	55–59	60–64	65–69	70–74	75–79	80–84	85–89
1914	25	78	121	85	68	90	109	122	70	56	192	6	8	1	..
1915	20	91	76	80	70	93	89	127	71	57	30	11	10	2	..
1916	22	188	156	109	101	135	143	164	83	95	33	29	10	1	..
1917	30	116	91	109	73	119	87	129	110	91	51	13	13	1	1
1918	32	88	106	106	104	60	89	117	66	62	41	25	7	1	..
1919	26	113	152	181	104	113	126	163	129	130	50	27	19	3	..
1920	14	106	149	132	86	97	97	131	100	113	55	33	5	2	..
1921	32	130	165	139	63	97	74	113	91	90	44	16	13	3	2
1922	19	98	130	111	71	67	78	68	57	93	45	25	9	3	1
1923	17	139	213	212	111	167	107	101	80	89	44	44	14	4	4
1924	28	79	227	170	140	128	113	116	75	145	53	24	19	16	1
1925	40	175	266	229	165	160	98	137	102	142	66	41	36	3	1
1926	37	136	237	226	147	128	127	99	82	75	62	45	36	7	3
1927	75	238	354	340	273	190	181	132	95	106	56	25	17	2	..

The highest frequency of arrests occurred in the age group 25–29, comprising 14.0 per cent of the total number reporting ages, and the second highest is the group 30–34, comprising 11.0 per cent. The smallest numbers arrested were in the groups 15–19, comprising 2.7 per cent of the total reporting age, and in the groups from 70 years upward. But, beginning with the group 20–24, through the group 60–64, there is an almost even proportion in the distribution of arrests among all the age groups; there is not one in which there occurred a notably higher number of arrests. Thus: the age group 20–24 has 11.3 per cent of the total reporting age; the 25–29 group has 14.0 per cent; the 30–34 group has 13.0 per cent; the 35–39 group has 9.1 per cent; the 40–44 group has 9.4 per cent; the 45–49 group has 8.7 per cent; the 50–54 group has 9.9 per cent; the 55–59 group has 6.9 per cent; and the 60–64 group has 7.8 per cent. An appreciable decrease in the older age groups occurs only in the 65–69, 70–74, and 75–79 age groups, being 3.7 per cent, 2.1 per cent, and 1.2 per cent, respectively.

The following explanation may be offered in an effort to interpret the trend of these Chinese arrests: (1) The habit of "taking a chance" at lotteries is possessed by the old and the young; about half of the Chinese arrests were occasioned by this state offense, which means that young and old in the Chinese communities participate in lotteries. (2) Gambling is responsible for almost another quarter of the Chinese arrests; and gaming with cards or other devices is another form of lottery or game-of-chance to which the Chinese are accustomed and which they have been brought up to consider as recreation. Because of Chinese segregation in American life these Old-World habits have tended to be perpetuated from old to young; though some change is evidently occurring, as indicated in Tables 61–63.

Examination of conditions in a representative Oriental community gives further witness. Table 61 shows the ages at which Chinese were arrested for lottery-playing (promoting, selling, buying, possessing tickets) in the city of Los Angeles, for which there is fullest data, and which may be taken as a sample of typical conditions in this respect.

TABLE 61

FREQUENCY OF CHINESE ARRESTS FOR LOTTERY-PLAYING, BY AGE GROUPS, CITY OF LOS ANGELES POLICE RECORDS, 1914–1927

Year	15–19	20–24	25–29	30–34	35–39	40–44	45–49	50–54	55–59	60–64	65–69	70–74	75–79	80–84	85–89
1914	3	17	37	32	26	21	36	32	8	3	..	2	..	1	..
1915	..	17	15	23	29	30	16	28	13	5	3	1	..	..	..
1916	..	35	77	48	48	50	64	55	19	21	8	3	1	..	..
1917	..	26	20	15	29	23	30	31	23	15	2	2	..	..	..
1918	..	25	42	37	42	20	40	54	30	17	11	7	5	1	..
1919	..	41	61	86	53	39	54	66	58	50	18	12	7	..	..
1920	1	53	85	82	43	41	58	53	58	58	26	12	1	..	..
1921	1	38	46	44	26	24	22	46	30	29	10	5	5	1	..
1922	2	17	42	35	36	24	25	30	13	27	11	13	1	..	1
1923	..	29	41	50	30	27	28	33	22	17	3	3	..	..	..
1924	1	48	94	64	45	50	43	44	21	42	7	1	3	..	1
1925	7	68	119	72	77	60	39	53	28	25	10	9	..	..	..
1926	1	33	74	45	34	29	29	31	16	8	2	2	2	..	..
1927	9	73	126	131	81	50	43	44	28	28	15	5	1	1	..
Total	25	520	879	764	599	488	527	600	375	345	126	77	26	4	2

It is seen that arrests for lottery-playing are made from among all age groups beginning with 20 years (25 occur at still younger ages), and commence to decline in volume after 65 years. With the exception of juveniles, all members of the community take part in lotteries, the large proportion of arrests being, as the records inform, for possessing lottery tickets or visiting what are either known to be or suspected of being lottery joints.

The ages of the Chinese arrested for gaming prove equally interesting. The largest numbers of arrests for gambling in Los Angeles are among those 60–64 years old (130) and among those 50–54 years (122), from 1914 to 1927. The third largest number of arrests were made in the age group 30–34 years (93), the fourth from the group 55–59 (88), and the fifth from the group 40–44 (78), in the total thirteen-year period. Thus arrests for gambling occur more frequently among the older, not the

TABLE 62

FREQUENCY OF CHINESE ARRESTS FOR GAMING BY AGE GROUPS, CITY OF LOS ANGELES POLICE RECORDS, 1914–1927

Year	15–19	20–24	25–29	30–34	35–39	40–44	45–49	50–54	55–59	60–64	65–69	70–74	75–79	80–84
1914	..	..	2	2	3	..	2	4	2	3	2	..	..	..
1915	..	..	..	..	..	..	..	..	..	..	..	..	..	..
1916	2	3	2	6	6	11	14	17	12	6	2	3	1	..
1917	3	4	2	6	2	4	7	14	1	5	1	..	..	..
1918	..	2	..	1	1	..	1	4	8	..	..	..	1	..
1919	..	4	1	4	1	6	10	12	7	16	4	1	..	..
1920	1	6	3	7	9	5	5	10	12	12	1	2	..	..
1921	..	3	2	7	5	5	2	12	2	12	7	..	2	..
1922	..	1	3	..	..	..	1	2	1	4	1	..	..	..
1923	..	..	..	..	..	..	..	1	11	1	..	6	..	..
1924	..	14	17	15	17	11	20	17	25	18	8	5	..	..
1925	..	16	15	22	13	23	3	23	..	46	14	2	2	1
1926	..	2	5	9	6	5	4	4	5	2	1	..	..	..
1927	2	7	13	14	8	8	..	2	2	5	1	1	1	..
Total ..	8	62	65	93	71	78	69	122	88	130	42	20	7	1

younger, Chinese. It is of interest to note that for gambling offenses among the age groups 20–65, the group 20–24 occasioned the smallest number of arrests (viz., 62), throughout the thirteen-year period 1914–1927, and that the number of offenses for gambling among the 14–19 age group is almost negligible (8).

For violation of opium and other narcotic laws, the arrests occurred as shown, by age groups, in Table 63.

The highest frequencies of arrests for violations of the narcotics laws are in the age groups 30–34, 25–29, and 45–49; followed by the groups 40–44, 50–54, 55–59, 35–39, and 60–64. The lowest number of arrests for this offense are among the groups 15–24 and 65–79. In other words, the very young and the very old, seem exempt. It is to be observed, however, that the special age character of the Chinese population of California has peculiar significance in explaining the small number of arrests found among the very young and the relatively aged as given in the preceding tables. The Chinese population as a whole is steadily decreasing,[1] the total number reaching the upper ages is small, and the number of children and youth is also dwindling. In other words the age composition of the Chinese in California does not parallel the more normal composition in regard to age distribution, this being the result of the exclusion legislation and also the social policy of segregation under which they live.

---

[1] Census returns for 1930 suggest that this tendency has ended.

TABLE 63

FREQUENCY OF CHINESE ARRESTS FOR VIOLATIONS OF OPIUM AND OTHER
NARCOTIC LAWS, BY AGE GROUPS, CITY OF LOS ANGELES
POLICE RECORDS, 1914–1927

Year	15–19	20–24	25–29	30–34	35–39	40–44	45–49	50–54	55–59	60–64	65–69	70–74	75–79
1914	..	1	6	3	3	9	7	6	13	10	1	..	4
1915	..	3	2	3	3	7	6	5	4	3	1	1	4
1916	..	9	9	9	11	14	14	17	2	13	..	4	1
1917	1	4	6	6	12	10	9	13	9	12	10	2	4
1918	..	8	7	8	13	5	8	11	11	6	3	..	..
1919	..	7	9	12	12	8	9	6	6	1	1	1	..
1920	1	5	6	12	2	11	7	16	10	4	3	..	..
1921	..	1	9	5	1	5	4	10	4	1	2	..	..
1922	..	..	6	7	2	9	3	7	3	7	1	..	1
1923	..	4	7	12	6	6	9	6	9	8	7	3	3
1924	..	3	20	7	4	6	6	1	7	9	6	..	..
1925	1	1	14	17	5	8	15	..	4	8	2	2	1
1926	1	1	2	10	4	3	9	1	2	1	1	1	2
1927	..	3	13	7	6	4	5	3	3	3	..	1	..
Total	4	50	116	118	86	105	111	102	87	86	38	15	20

It is of interest to see on the other hand at what ages arrests and commitments to penal institutions occurred among both the Chinese and the Japanese, for the graver offenses such as homicide, assault, robbery, burglary, and so forth. The following table shows the distribution of ages of the Chinese committed to San Quentin Prison, 1914–1927:

TABLE 64

AGE PERIODS OF CHINESE COMMITTED TO SAN QUENTIN PRISON, 1914–1927

Year	15–19	20–24	25–29	30–34	35–39	40–44	45–49	50–54	55–59	60–64	65–69	70–74	75–79	80–84	90–94
1914	1	3	6	4	1	..	2	..	3	..	..	..	..	..	..
1915	1	5	1	2	..	1	..	..	..	..	..	..	..	..	..
1916	1	3	1	..	1	1	1	..	1	2	..	..	..	..	..
1917	1	4	3	2	1	..	..	..	1	2	..	..	..	..	..
1918	3	4	4	3	1	..	..	1	..	1	..	..	..	..	..
1919	1	2	2	..	1	..	..	..	..	..	..	..	..	..	..
1920	..	4	1	1	1	..	2	..	..	..	..	..	..	..	1
1921	..	4	2	2	1	2	..	1	..	..	..	..	..	..	..
1922	1	5	5	5	1	2	2	1	1	2	..	..	..	..	..
1923	1	3	2	1	1	2	6	1	1	2	1	2	..	1	..
1924	..	2	2	1	1	1	2	..	1	..	2	..	..	..	..
1925	..	..	..	4	1	..	..	1	1	1	2	..	..	..	..
1926	..	5	4	2	2	1	..	..	..	1	..	1	..	..	..
1927	..	7	3	2	2	3	1	..	..	..	..	..	..	..	..
Total	10	51	36	29	15	13	16	5	9	11	5	3	..	1	1

The largest numbers of commitments to San Quentin during the period 1914–1927 were from among the age groups 20–34 years; of these three groups, the highest number, 51, was in the group 20–24, the second largest, 36, in the group 25–29, and the third largest, in the group 30–34, was 29 commitments. Possibly this is due to the tong activities for which are engaged the youthful "highbinders." An examination of the ages of those committed for murder, first and second degree, seems to indicate such a possibility.

The table below shows the ages of Chinese committed to San Quentin for first- and second-degree murder:

TABLE 65

NUMBER OF CHINESE COMMITTED TO SAN QUENTIN PRISON FOR FIRST- AND SECOND-DEGREE MURDER, BY AGE GROUPS, 1914–1927

Year	15–19	20–24	25–29	30–34	35–39	40–44	45–49	50–54	55–59	60–64	65–69	70–74
1914	..	1	2	2	..	..	..	..	..	..	..	..
1915	..	2	3	..	..	..	..	..	..	..	..	..
1916	1	2	..	..	..	..	..	..	..	..	..	..
1917	..	2	..	1	..	..	..	..	..	..	..	..
1918	1	..	2	1	1	..	..	1	..	..	..	..
1919	1	3	1	..	..	..	1	..	..	..	..	..
1920	..	4	2	..	..	..	..	..	..	..	..	..
1921	..	3	1	..	..	..	1	1	1	1	..	..
1922	1	4	4	2	..	1	..	1	..	..	..	..
1923	..	1	..	..	..	..	..	..	..	..	..	..
1924	..	..	..	1	..	..	1	..	1	..	..	..
1925	..	..	..	1	..	..	..	..	..	..	..	..
1926	..	..	..	..	..	..	..	..	..	..	..	..
1927	..	..	1	..	..	..	...	..	..	..	..	..
Total	4	22	16	8	1	1	3	3	2	1	0	0

As seen above, the most frequent commitments of Chinese for murder occurred in the age groups 20 to 34 years, and comprise in each case almost half of the total commitments in these age groups at San Quentin. Thus, the total number in the group 20–24 sent to San Quentin during 1914–1927 is 51, of which 22 were on the charge of murder; in the group 25–29 there were 36, of which 16 were for murder; in the group 30–34, the total number committed was 29, of which 8 were for murder; the total number in the group 15–19 was 10, of which 4 were for murder. The older groups appear less for murder, and more for other offenses of personal violence, gainful offenses, and the graver offenses against public policy.

The age groups of Japanese giving age data committed to San Quentin Prison, according to the prison records, during the period 1914 to 1927 appear below:

TABLE 66

NUMBER OF JAPANESE COMMITTED TO SAN QUENTIN PRISON, BY AGE GROUPS, 1914–1927

Year	15–19	20–24	25–29	30–34	35–39	40–44	45–49	50–54	55–59
1914	1	..	4	1	1	..	..	..	..
1915	1	3	3	2	..	1	..	..	..
1916	..	..	3	..	1	..	..	..	1
1917	..	..	..	..	2	..	..	1	..
1918	..	..	1	2	..	..	..	..	..
1919	..	2	..	..	2	1	..	..	..
1920	..	1	1	2	1	1	1	..	..
1921	..	..	..	1	1	2	..	..	..
1922	..	1	2	4	4	1	..	..	..
1923	..	3	1	2	2	..	..	..	..
1924	..	..	2	..	1	..	..	..	..
1925	..	1	..	..	2	..	..	..	1
1926	..	1	..	1	..	1	..	..	..
1927	..	..	..	1	..	2	..	..	..
Total	2	12	17	16	17	9	1	1	2

Here the higher frequency in the commitment of crimes occurs in the four age groups, 20–24, 25–29, 30–34, and 35–39. The largest number is found in the groups 25–40 years: 17 commitments in the group 25–29, 16 in the group 30–34, and 17 in the group 35–39; whereas among the Chinese the largest number of commitments occurred in the two groups 20–24, 25–29. There are but two commitments under 20, and 13 over the age of 40, and none at all over the age of 60. The crimes which occasioned the highest frequency of commitments among the Japanese are forgery, circulating fictitious checks, murder, and manslaughter.

VII. CONCLUSION

In concluding this study of Oriental crime in California, it is essential to bear in mind the usual distinction[1] between the more serious social offenses or "crimes" and those which, while not unimportant, are less serious. The legal code itself recognizes this difference, expressing it through greater and less severity of punishment. The more serious offenses are, on the whole, those recognized as such not only in our own law but in the penal systems of most other civilizations. These offenses are therefore fairly well recognized and are imbedded in the culture patterns of individuals of varying cultural backgrounds and geographical habitats. Such a statement needs some modification for certain particular offenses for a few peoples. Yet it fairly well describes a general situation. Murder, theft, arson, rape, and the like are thought of as serious offenses against social welfare and are so rated in the culture patterns of most peoples today. Hence, on the whole, immigrants from any part of the world may be expected to recognize them as such, though, as has been said, there are some exceptions.

But usages in regard to acts of less serious social consequence vary from one part of the world to another. What is acceptable and even commendable in one culture may be forbidden in another. Immigrants are carriers of those culture patterns which belong to their own people. They come as culture strangers to a new world, and their "assimilation" in the new life is a process of culture modification; it is a process of adaptation through learning the "ways" about them. This process, like all learning, is a slow one, demanding time and favorable conditions. Hence it is in the range of the large variety of lesser "crimes" or offenses that aliens may be expected to be found as offenders against the law.

In this respect Oriental immigrants do not differ from other aliens in the United States. Their offenses, as indicated in this study of commitments and arrests, are the consequences primarily of failure to observe city ordinances and similar state enactments, an understanding of which their very newness to American life makes difficult. Probably the most obvious fact brought out in this study of Orientals is that their behavior, in so far as it has involved the breaking of legal enactments, has run in the same channels and exhibited the same characteristics as the behavior of other aliens. For the larger part of their offenses are not of major im-

---

[1] Reference may be made to the *California Penal Code*, Sections 16 and 17, *California Jurisprudence*, Vol. VII, and *Criminal Law*, p. 870, Section IV.

portance. They are offenses classed as misdemeanors, part of them, at least, probably resulting from ignorance of the existence of such laws or from a lack of understanding of what is meant by them. In respect to more serious crimes the record of these races in California is better than might be expected rather than worse, only a very small percentage of their offenses belonging in this category. As compared with offenders of the white race they stand reasonably high.

Only a few items need to be given to illustrate this general conclusion: during the entire period 1900–1927 there was a total of 71,626 Chinese arrests, of which 1,028 were for crimes punishable by death or by imprisonment in the two state prisons, San Quentin and Folsom. The figures for the Japanese for the same period are a total of 17,727 arrests, 382 involving death or imprisonment in state prisons. Represented in percentages, 1.44 per cent of the Chinese offenses and 2.2 per cent of the Japanese offenses were of this more serious character. During the period of this study (1900–1927) the total of all commitments to San Quentin was 55,509, of which 978 were Chinese (1.8 per cent) and 364 were Japanese (0.7 per cent). For Folsom the total commitments were 10,410, of which 50 (five-tenths of one per cent) were Chinese, and 18 (two-tenths of one per cent) were Japanese. These commitments represent serious offenses. During the same period, as listed in the centers studied, there was a total of 2,037,794 arrests of every sort and of all types of persons; 3.5 per cent were Chinese and 0.9 per cent were Japanese. The commitments to the two state prisons for serious offenses total 65,919, which amounts to 3.2 per cent of the total number of arrests. In other words, over a period of years from 1900 to 1927, out of the total of arrests for every sort of offense, serious or slight, running from murder to parking an automobile overtime, the entire body of serious offenders committed to state prisons constituted 3.2 per cent of the total. For the same period the Chinese serious offenders committed to State's prison constituted 1.44 per cent of the total Chinese offenses and the Japanese serious offenders constituted 2.2 per cent of the total Japanese offenses. It is evident that the Oriental serious offenses in relation to total Oriental offenses are low—lower than the average for the state as a whole—and that the absolute total of Oriental serious offenses is but a small fraction of the entire number of such offenses committed by men of all races in the state.

It is of interest also to note that a study of the commitments to San Quentin (where the records cover a larger total than those at Folsom) reveals a difference between the two Oriental peoples in regard to the increase or decrease of their prison commitments in relation to the changing size of their population in California. The Chinese population in California decreased steadily from 1900 to 1920 (37 per cent). The Chinese in San

Quentin numbered considerably less in 1910 than in 1900, but between 1910 and 1920 there was a considerable increase, though the number is smaller than in 1900. On the whole there is a decrease of commitments between 1900 and 1920 (25.8 per cent), paralleling the decrease in population, but the rate of decrease in commitments is smaller than the rate of population decrease. By contrast, the Japanese population in California increased greatly (over 600 per cent) between 1900 and 1920; but the rate of increase in the number of the Japanese committed to San Quentin was very much less (33.6 per cent) than the rate of population increase.

On the whole, the following considerations seem to be evident: A considerable percentage of offenses committed by Orientals is found among the minor offenses and evidences a lack of acquaintance with the ways—the culture—of America. This fact is clear in regard to both Oriental groups. As a general rule, aliens in process of assimilation, especially in the earlier years, seem regularly to show this same situation, and these two peoples do not differ from other immigrants in this respect.

A further condition to be considered as an explanatory factor is the unusual percentage of males to females. This was for a time true of each of the Oriental groups, but in time became less true of the Japanese, while still remaining a marked characteristic of Chinese life in America.[1] The influence upon social life of unbalanced sex distribution seems to be usually associated with some degree of social disorder and irregularity. It may have been of considerable influence in regard especially to the Chinese. The historic basis of the inequality in their case is primarily the legislative position forced upon the Chinese by the long period of exclusion, while a similar position for the Japanese has had a much shorter duration.

Probably of great consequence also is the segregation aspect of American life for Orientals. The basis of this segregation is cultural conflict, resting upon custom variations and ending in legislative limitations. The segregation situation differs as between the two peoples. Among the Chinese it has a much longer history, and the discriminations against them are of much longer standing. Moreover, China, as a nation, has never been in a position to make effective protest. Hence for the Chinese settlers a simpler process seemed to be to find a way of life within their own culture and within narrow limits in residence, occupations, and social activities. The effort on their part in the direction of assimilation has therefore tended to be defeated by the situation itself, and hence arose clashes or conflicts from time to time between the two cultures, as expressed in individual be-

---

[1] It should be remarked that the records of Chinese life in the United States during the most recent years (1925–1930) also indicate a gradual change toward a more normal distribution between the sexes.

havior. And at the same time there has been a persistence of those minor offenses which usually are the result of lack of understanding by the recent alien, but should, under favorable contacts and the intermingling of life, soon decrease or disappear. The importance of extreme segregation in respect to the Chinese in regard to criminal record is very great and merits further study.

The Japanese, on the contrary, have steadily refused to accept segregated life, in either residence or occupations. Their immigration became relatively large at a time during which the Japanese nation was coming to have a place among nations. This fact is reflected in the tendency of their nationals here to try to gain a place in California comparable to that of European aliens in the United States. Hence they show less of the segregated life, either in residence or occupations, than do the Chinese. They have more eagerly sought avenues of contact and influences of assimiliation, and they have attempted to avoid conflict. Probably this marked difference between them as residents of California is of vital importance in explaining the considerable difference between the criminal records of the two Oriental peoples. For these differences are all social-historical; they concern culture contacts, and are evidently in no sense racial.

INDEX

Age groups, 12–13
Ages of Oriental offenders analyzed, 83–91
Alameda County arrests, 35
Arrests: variation in records of, 6, 23; volume and percentages of, summarized, 51–53; *see also* Offenses

Bercovici, Konrad, 69, 70
Berkeley, Oriental arrests in, 47–48
Boddy, E. M., 82

California Penal Code, 92
Chinatown, San Francisco's, 27
Chinese: arrests, by age groups, 86–90; offenses analyzed, 62
City ordinances, violation of, 59, 70, 71
Commitments to state prisons, 23–26
Coolidge, M. R., 68, 69, 72, 82
Crime, *see* Arrests, Offenses
Criminal conduct related to cultural background, 64

Disturbing the peace, 72
Divorces, 12
Drunkenness, 72

Fairchild, Henry Pratt, 71
Federal Commission on Immigration, 54, 71
Folsom Prison, 38, 93
Fresno County arrests, 33, 34, 43–44

Gambling, 67–68
Gaming and lottery, 59
General conclusions, 92–95
Geographical distribution of Oriental population, 14–22

Immigration Commission, Federal, 54, 71
Immigration laws, violation of, 71
Imperial County arrests, 34, 35, 45
Industry of Orientals, 82

Japanese: arrests, by age groups, 84–85; juvenile delinquency slight, 85; offenses analyzed, 63–64, 73–75

Kern County arrests, 46–47

Liquor laws, violation of, 59
Los Angeles arrests, 28–29, 39
Lottery offenses, 59, 65–66

McKenzie, R. D., 65
Marital condition of Orientals, 12
Method of investigation, 5
Mitchell, Edmund, 68

Oakland arrests, 29, 40
Occupations of Oriental offenders analyzed, 77–82
Offenses: against the person, 56, 57; against property, 61; against public policy and morals, 57, 58, 59, 66–67; against public health and safety, 60, 61; types of, analyzed, 54–76
Opium and narcotics laws, violation of, 59
Oriental arrest percentages summarized, 48–51
Oriental distribution in California described, 9–20; changes in male population, 10–11; female population increase, 10–11; settlement, centers of, 18–22

Park, Robert G., 7
Penal Code classification, 54, 55
Physical marks of race, and assimilation, 7
Prisoners in 1923, *Census Special Report,* 73–76
Prostitution, 72

Racial segregation, 7
Ratio of Oriental males to females, 94
Reynolds, C. N., 73

Sacramento City and County arrests, 30–33, 40–43
San Francisco arrests, 38, 39
San Joaquin County arrests, 45
San Jose arrests, 31–32, 40–41

[97